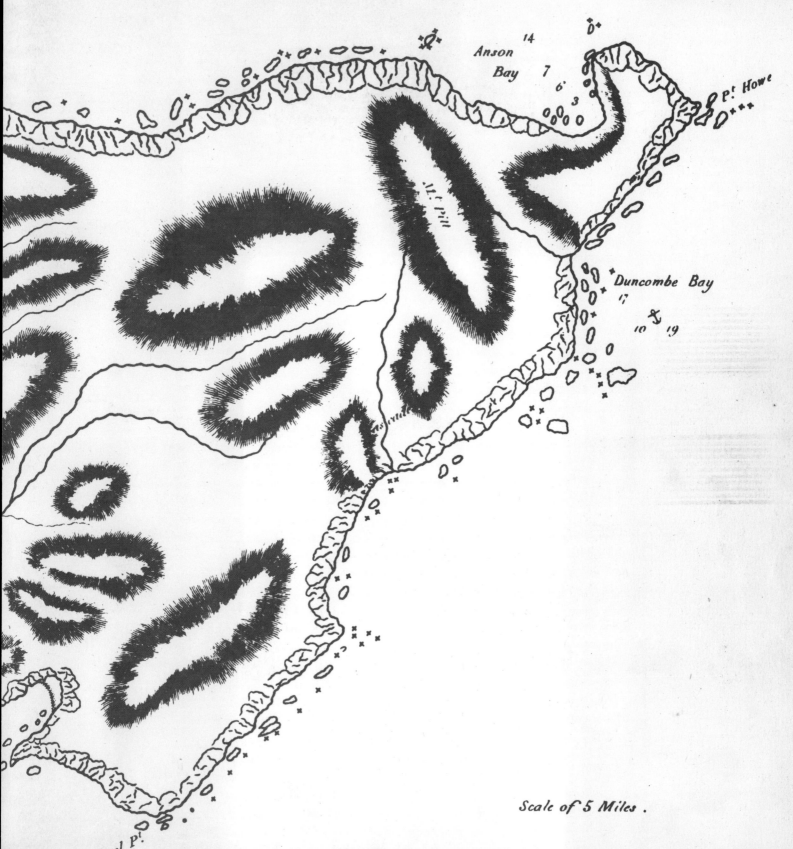

Anson Bay

14

7

6

3

Pt Howe

Mt Pitt

Duncombe Bay

17

10   19

Scale of 5 Miles.

Steel Pt

03

Hell and Paradise

VIKING

Near the watering place, Matavai — Island of O'tahytey ... 1792

THE NORFOLK · BOUNTY · PITCAIRN SAGA

Hell and Paradise

PETER CLARKE

Picture sources: *Illustrative material from England (National Maritime Museum, National Portrait Gallery and Public Record Office), from France (The Louvre), from the Isle of Man (Manx Museum), and from the National Library of Australia, the Royal Australian Historical Society and the State Library of Victoria is separately acknowledged. The Christian and Price family crests, and maps of the Pacific taken from Captain de Surville's memoirs and A.R. Fremin's 'Océanie', have been reproduced with the kind permission of the syndics of the Cambridge University Library. Crown copyright material in the Public Record Office is reproduced by permission of the Controller of Her Majesty's Stationery Office. All other pictorial matter, except for contemporary photography, is from the Mitchell and Dixson Libraries in Sydney, Australia, to the staff of which the author is deeply grateful. The colour photographs of Norfolk Island were taken by Ron Thompson of AdVertisements, Melbourne, with the exception of a few taken by the author. The Pitcairn colour shots were the work of Tom Lloyd, editor of the 'Norfolk Islander' and one of the 'Pitcairn Pilgrims'.*

Every effort has been made to trace the original source of all material and the publishers would be grateful to hear from copyright holders to rectify any omission.

Author's note: *My heartfelt thanks go to Doctors Jim and Milly Cerini for meticulous and dedicated pictorial research on my behalf. And to my friend, Coral Aikin, who convinced me that all this was possible by early forays into the Mitchell Library. Thank you, too, Helen Duffy, for much early advice and, again, Ron Thompson, for design work when it appeared the book would be produced in Australia.*

My crazily-expensive determination to have every double page spread reward the reader with pictures which match the text would have been impossible without the talent and dedication of Optimus Graphic Design of London, Cambridge, Sydney and Melbourne, led by my dynamic and devoted friend, Brian Grainger. It was a pleasure to work alongside Jon Martin, a fine, sensitive art director, and, in person and by 'fax', Arvo Podersoo, a loving editor. To Peter Denniss who supervised the artwork, and Steve Hawes and Andy Roberts, who worked with him; to Andrew Le Mottée for typographical control; to Pattie Lamb for the lettering of the chapter headings; to Heather Pedley for historical research; and to Gill Almond, Jeremy Perrott and everyone at Optimus – my thanks for help when I badly needed it.

Contents

Chapter

1	Botany Bay to Norfolk	9
2	Captain Bligh and Mr. Christian	19
3	Paradise Found	31
4	Prologue to Mutiny	41
5	The Eruption	45
6	The 8000 Mile Quest	55
7	Pursuit	63
8	Commandants and Convicts	67
9	William Bligh Again	77
10	Purgatory in Eden	83
11	The Evangelisation of Pitcairn	91
12	Second Settlement – Norfolk	103
13	Fresh Blood	111
14	Seduction of the Innocents	121
15	Reform and Reaction on Norfolk	131
16	For the Term of His Natural Life	139
17	Pitcairn to Norfolk	145
18	'God's Gentlemen' and Others	151

Appendixes

1	Norfolk and Pitcairn Today	167
2	Pitcairn's Laws	173
3	Who Owns Norfolk Island?	177

Bibliography	185
Index	187

*Inside front cover: Norfolk Island – W. N.
Chapman. From 'The Voyage of Governor Phillip
to Botany Bay', published by John Stockdale
Half-title: Cat-o'-nine-tails – from a Dixson
Library display 'All in a day's work'
Title page: 'Near the watering place, Matavai.
Island of Otahytey' – George Tobin
Imprint and Introduction (background): Plans of
the 'Bounty' – National Maritime Museum, England;
(inset, top): H.M.S. 'Sirius' ('Safely moored in
Sidney Cove') – G. C. Ingleton;
(inset, bottom): H.M.S. 'Bounty' ('Sea Ruffians') –
G. C. Ingleton;
Contents (background): 'Convicts' – plate etched
by G. Bruce;
(inset): 'Convicts in chains at work' – Robert Jones's
notebook
Inside back cover: Carteret's chart of Pitcairn Island*

*Viking
Penguin Books Australia Ltd,
487 Maroondah Highway, PO Box 257, Ringwood,
Victoria, 3134, Australia
Penguin Books Ltd,
Harmondsworth, Middlesex, England
Viking Penguin Inc.,
40 West 23rd Street, New York, N.Y. 10010, U.S.A.
Penguin Books Canada Ltd,
2801 John Street, Markham, Ontario, Canada
L3R 1B4
Penguin Books (N.Z.) Ltd,
182-190 Wairau Road, Auckland 10, New Zealand*

First published 1986 by Viking

© Peter Clarke 1986

*Designed by Optimus Graphic Design
Cambridge · London · Melbourne · Sydney
Typesetting controlled by Interaction,
Cambridge, England. Typeset in England by
Ascender Graphics
Printed in Hong Kong by Mandarin Offset Ltd*

C|I|P

*Clarke, Peter, 1927-.
Hell and Paradise.*

*Bibliography.
Includes index.
ISBN 0 670 81521 7.*

*1. 'Bounty' (ship). 2. Norfolk Island – History.
3. Pitcairn Island – History. I. Title.*

994'. 82.

BOUNTY

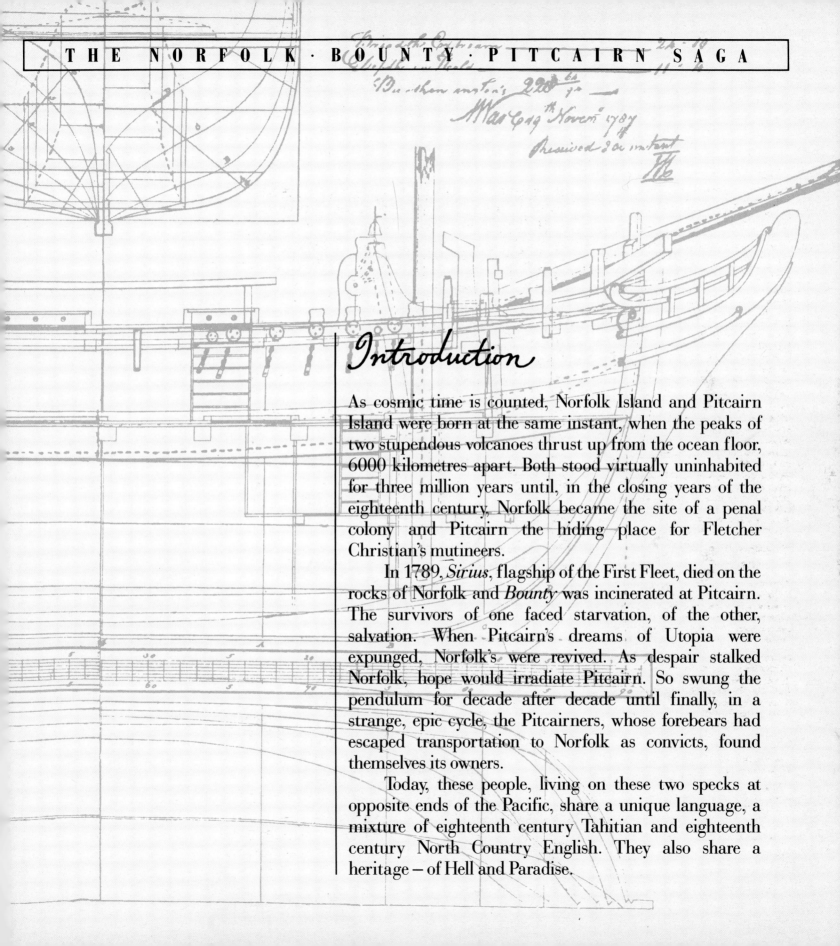

Introduction

As cosmic time is counted, Norfolk Island and Pitcairn Island were born at the same instant, when the peaks of two stupendous volcanoes thrust up from the ocean floor, 6000 kilometres apart. Both stood virtually uninhabited for three million years until, in the closing years of the eighteenth century, Norfolk became the site of a penal colony and Pitcairn the hiding place for Fletcher Christian's mutineers.

In 1789, *Sirius*, flagship of the First Fleet, died on the rocks of Norfolk and *Bounty* was incinerated at Pitcairn. The survivors of one faced starvation, of the other, salvation. When Pitcairn's dreams of Utopia were expunged, Norfolk's were revived. As despair stalked Norfolk, hope would irradiate Pitcairn. So swung the pendulum for decade after decade until finally, in a strange, epic cycle, the Pitcairners, whose forebears had escaped transportation to Norfolk as convicts, found themselves its owners.

Today, these people, living on these two specks at opposite ends of the Pacific, share a unique language, a mixture of eighteenth century Tahitian and eighteenth century North Country English. They also share a heritage — of Hell and Paradise.

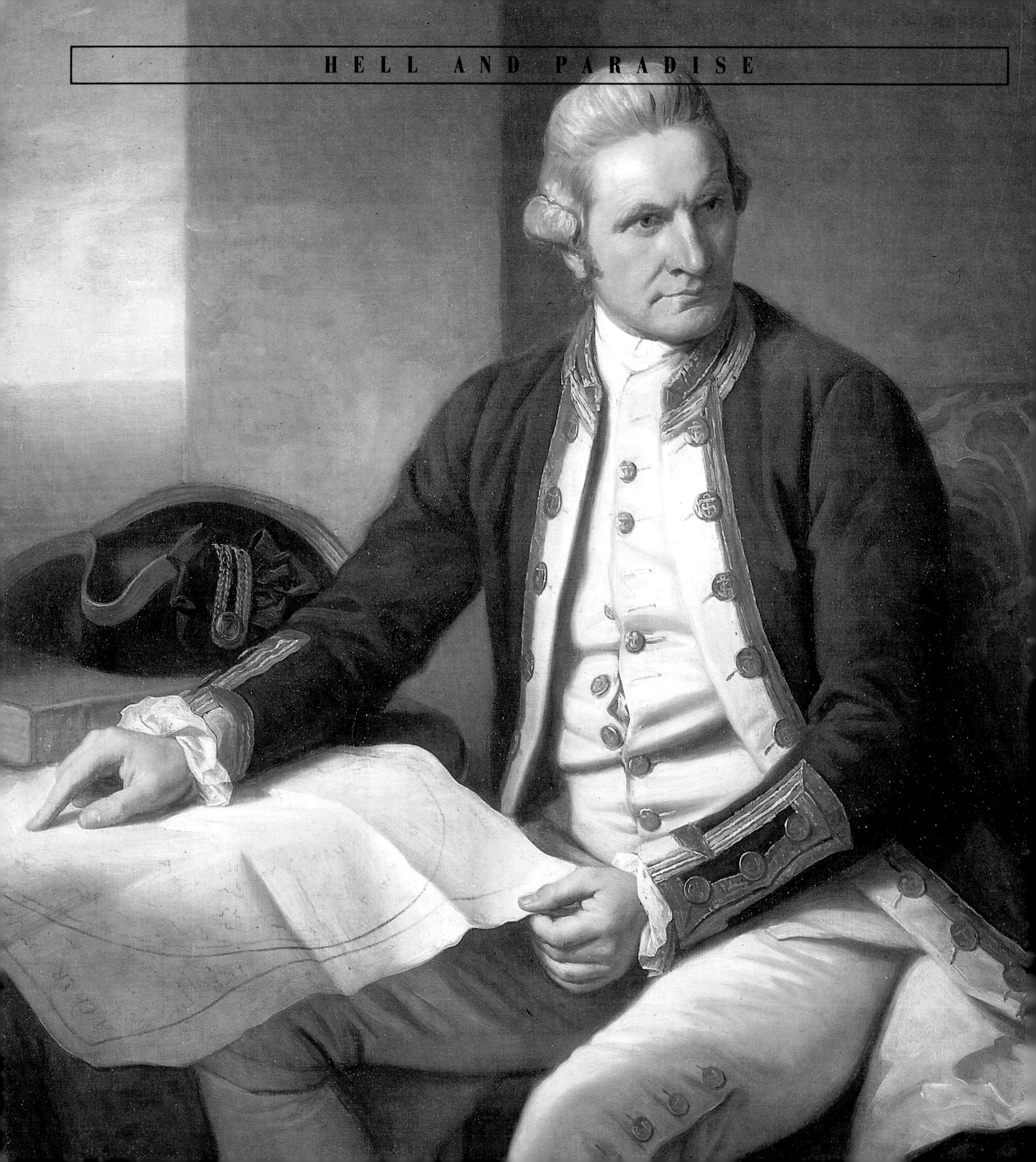

CHAPTER 1

Botany Bay to Norfolk

On the 19th of January, 1788, the First Fleet dropped anchor at Botany Bay. Its human cargo, which had been transported for crimes ranging from murder to 'stealing goods valued at a shilling or more', had spent eight months manacled below decks. The men and women convicts were in appalling shape, but perfectly intact was the library of books carefully chosen to cure their psychic ills. There were 200 copies of *Dissuasions from Stealing*, 200 copies of *Exercises against Lying* and 50 copies of *Caution to Swearers*.

Commander of the Fleet, Captain Arthur Phillip, was not impressed with Captain Cook's choice of site for a settlement and quickly decided to seek a more propitious one. Further up the coast, he probed an inlet whose potential Cook, uncharacteristically, had missed. Phillip called it 'the finest harbour in the world, in which a thousand sail of the line may ride in the most perfect security'. He named it Sydney Cove but the town he founded there he called Albion. The name just refused to stick and, about a year later, it became known as Sydney.

Six women convicts were destined never to set foot in The Great South Land. They were kept on board pending the carrying out of instructions contained in a letter to Phillip from Lord Sydney:

Norfolk Island being represented as a spot which may hereafter become useful, you are, as soon as circumstances admit it, to send a small establishment thither to secure the same to us and prevent it being occupied by subjects of any other European Power.

Captain Cook had discovered Norfolk whilst he was sailing the *Resolution* from New Caledonia to New Zealand in 1774. Patronage being the lifeblood of exploration, he named the island after the Duchess of Norfolk, wife of Howard, the premier peer of the realm. Cook described it as a 'Paradise', a word he had not used before in all his journeys.

Far left: Captain James Cook – Sir Nathaniel Dance. National Maritime Museum, England
Left: Captain Arthur Phillip – F. Wheatley, 1788
Above: Sydney Cove, 1788 – William Bradley
Below: 'Botany Bay: "Sirius" and Convoy going in' – William Bradley, 1788

'We are undoubtedly the first to set foot on it', Cook wrote and, for once, he was slightly wrong. Subsequent diggings revealed stone adzes and other implements which suggest that roving Polynesians once used Norfolk as a brief stop-over point. For some reason, the Polynesians never decided to settle on this benign island. No trace of permanent habitation has ever been found. Historians now believe that from the time it erupted from the sea, Norfolk Island stood virtually empty for millions of years.

Captain Cook took soundings throughout his voyage and correctly deduced that Norfolk and its two satellite islands are part of a gigantic chain of mountains (now called the Norfolk Ridge) stretching 1770 kilometres from New Caledonia to New Zealand. So deep is the sea that only these three peaks project. Their slopes plunge down through one of the Pacific's most fearful gulfs for a stupendous ten kilometres, making Norfolk's Mount Pitt, in a sense, higher than Mount Everest.

Cook was entranced by the colossal pine trees which smothered the island and which at the time existed only in this spot in the entire world. Britain was then engaged in the American War of Independence and her supplies of timber for shipbuilding and flax for sails were almost exhausted. Cook, ever the faithful servant of Empire, enthusiastically reported that timber and flax grew abundantly on Norfolk. His Majesty's Government had a further reason for colonising Norfolk – if the British didn't, the French would.

To lead the pioneering party and become Norfolk's first Commandant, Governor Phillip chose an officer well known to him – Lieutenant Philip Gidley King. The son of a moderately

Above: Lieutenant Philip Gidley King – about 1790
Right: Norfolk Pines at Sydney Bay – detail of a picture by William Bradley, 1790. Their resistance to salt air has led to Norfolk Pines being planted on beaches around the world. Every one, from Manly to Mombasa, has its origin on this tiny island.
Far right: Chart of Norfolk Island by William Bradley

well-to-do draper, King had come up through the Navy the hard way, entering as a captain's servant at the age of 12, becoming a midshipman after five years and brilliantly passing his officer's examinations three years later. On becoming a lieutenant, he had served under Phillip for five years.

King began recruiting the day after the First Fleet arrived. He would have moved with even more haste had he realised that the French at that very moment were endeavouring to land on Norfolk. The women were selected by the Ship's Surgeon as being 'the six whose characters stood fairest'. Choosing the men was a more difficult task but eventually nine convicts and eight free men were picked, their ages ranging from 16 to 72.

The oldest, Richard Widdicombe, had been a farmer. He was convicted for 'stealing one wooden winch and other goods, value four guineas', and was sentenced to seven years' transportation. The youngest, Charles McLennan, was convicted when he was only 14 and given seven years for 'stealing a bladder purse, value one penny, one gold half-guinea, one half-crown, and six pennies'. Of the motley 759 persons who arrived with the First Fleet, these 23 were selected as 'the best of a bad lot'.

In a remarkably short eight days, King had completed all arrangements and H.M.S. *Supply* sailed out into the vast South Pacific Ocean on a thousand mile journey to an island measuring five miles by three.

Norfolk Island was sighted at 11 a.m. on the 29th of February and for five days the vessel sailed to different points around the coast, endeavouring to find a place to land. Just six weeks earlier, the great French explorer, La Perouse, had found landing beyond him. He described it as a place fit only for 'angels and eagles'. Lieutenant King began to share this view.

Faced everywhere with surf-lashed cliffs up to 300 feet high, he managed to secure a toe-hold at a couple of spots but found nowhere suitable for the landing of a large party. 'I now began to think it was impossible to land on ye isle', he wrote, but eventually, at a spot King

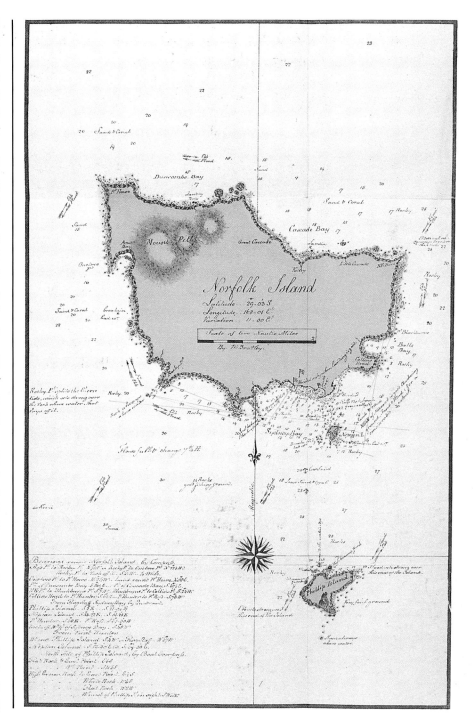

named Sydney Bay, his Ship's Master discovered a channel through the reef sufficiently wide to allow the passage of the larger launches, the longboat and the pinnace.

Notwithstanding the fact that Captain Cook had claimed the island for Britain in 1774, King went through the ceremony again, formalising Norfolk as Britain's second possession in the Pacific, less than six weeks after the proclamation of the first, New South Wales. As that colony's town was not yet known by the illustrious name of Sydney, he bestowed it on his tent town.†

He drank a toast to His Majesty, to the Queen, to the Prince of Wales and to 'Success to the Settlement', after which three cheers were given.

Within a few days, it seemed that success was not impossible. The First Settlement was not designed as a dumping ground for convicts. It was to be the garden which would feed the struggling, barren settlement back in Australia. It was to be the source of great pine masts for His Majesty's ships and of flax for their sails. Already, they had seen evidence to confirm George Forster's account of 'trees as thick as two men could fathom' and 'birds infinitely more brilliant than in New Zealand', including rails and pigeons, the latter 'the largest in the world'.‡ The volcanic soil seemed rich, the sea seethed with fish, the climate was balmy, if a little warm for an Englishman's taste.

In such a place, even hardened felons might mellow. And, in any event, escape was impossible. An early convict or two might be tempted to try swimming to Nepean Island, just half a mile offshore. But should he manage to get rid of his irons and, by great good fortune, strike a day when the usual frothing cauldron was just a nasty swell, and should he find a foothold on the snarling rocks, enabling him to clamber ashore, he would find nothing to eat — unless he could catch a sea-bird with his bare hands — and, worse, nothing to drink.

Should an exceptionally desperate wretch make it through the ferocious rips to Phillip Island††, four miles away, he would find the

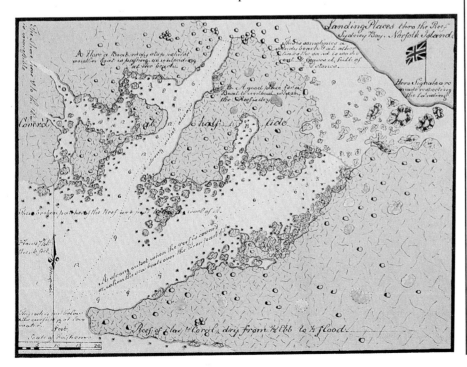

† *It was later to be changed to Kingston, then to King's Town. With the arrival of the Pitcairners, it was slurred back to Kingston.*
‡ *The brothers Forster were recruited by Cook after Sir Joseph Banks withdrew from the voyage, one assumes in something of a huff, when Cook refused to allow the building of a top-heavy cabin which Banks proposed to house himself, his plants and his entourage.*
†† *Phillip Island was named after Sydney's first Governor, Captain Arthur Phillip. Somewhere down the years, one 'l' was lost and the island is now known as Philip Island.*

island teeming with edible sea-birds, including Masked Boobies whose chicks outweigh their parents. If it was not the birds' breeding season, however, hunger would eventually drive him to an attempt to catch the pearly geckoes, and even the superb Wanderer butterflies, and finally the gigantic centipedes, a horrific 11 inches long. But probably he would not last that long for on the entire island he would find not a drop of drinkable water.

To ensure there would be no escape by boat, the Governor of New South Wales forbade the building on Norfolk of any vessel — by anyone — that was longer than twenty feet. It was probably a baroque worry. To reach New Caledonia in the north, the escapees would have

Below: Kneeling man being flogged
Right: The Settlement in 1790 —
G. Raper

needed to navigate some 400 miles. South-east, to New Zealand, was over 500 miles. And due west, to the spot where Byron Bay stands today, stretched 900 miles of trackless ocean.

By the standards of those times, Philip Gidley King was a relatively benign man and far worse were to follow him. A twentieth century mind, however, would find his methods blood-curdling. Six weeks after the landing, King meted out his first punishment. Seaman John Batchelor was accused of stealing rum from King's own tent and received three dozen lashes.†

Undeterred by being forced to watch the flogging of Batchelor, young Charles McLennan went on a rum search and found it in Surgeon Jamison's tent. For this he received 50 lashes. He had just recently turned 16.

The Commandant lost no time in taking a mistress, choosing an ex-dressmaker named Ann Inett who, for stealing a few clothes, had been sentenced to death by hanging, but reprieved and given seven years' transportation. Encouraged by King's example, Edward Garth, a young man who had also had his death sentence reprieved, paired off with Susannah Gough, an ex-prostitute, while Nathaniel Lucas, a carpenter, settled down with 25-year-old Olivia Gasgoin whose crime was rather more serious than the others — 'stealing with force and arms'. In a very short time, all three ladies were pregnant and a new generation was beginning, a people whose origins were in the South Pacific.

On the 8th of January, 1789, Ann Inett presented Commandant King with the settle-ment's first child, whom he proudly named *Norfolk*.

At this stage, King's instructions from the

Crown seemed possible of fulfilment. He had already constructed a road from Sydney (Kingston) to Anson Bay via Mount Pitt and made much headway in clearing ground, felling trees, and sawing wood for a variety of buildings. He had located a good source of limestone at the western end of Turtle Bay (now known as Emily) and thus had the ingredient for mortar and plaster. Kilns were constructed on the rock face overlooking Slaughter Bay. He had planted groves of Rio banana trees, orange trees, sugar cane, rice, wheat and barley, pumpkins, potatoes, turnips, artichokes, lettuce, onions, leeks, celery and parsley. The land was proving much more productive than that around Port Jackson. Hopes were high.

At the end of January came King's first insurrection. Some newly transported convicts from Port Jackson concocted an elaborate plan to capture the next ship to arrive at Norfolk and sail her to Tahiti. They were betrayed and the scheme nipped in the bud but it is interesting to contemplate what might have transpired had they been successful. They would have arrived in Tahiti whilst Captain Bligh's party was still there and, in all probability, been captured. When the *Bounty* sailed, her underdecks would have been crowded with desperate men under threat of death. Master/servant and moral/immoral relationships on board would have been so drastically changed that the world's most famous mutiny might never have occurred.

† *Batchelor was also the first to die. Just three months later, he was swept overboard on a fishing expedition and drowned.*

CHAPTER 2

Captain Bligh and Mr. Christian

While the *Sirius*, flagship of the First Fleet, was plying its miserable way to Botany Bay, a somewhat smaller ship was being equipped to play its role in history. She was H.M.S. *Bounty*, to be commanded by Captain William Bligh, aged 33. His Master's Mate was to be Fletcher Christian, just turned 23.

The purpose of the *Bounty*'s journey was to collect breadfruit plants from Tahiti and to transport them to the West Indies.

Much pious nonsense was disseminated about the use to which this wonder-plant was to be put: it was to be 'a boon to the poor of the world'. Even Boswell was impressed and asked Dr. Johnson to consider the difference between the traditional way of producing bread and this new way: 'no more plowing, no more sowing,

harrowing, reaping, threshing, baking!'

Bligh's commissioners were wealthy plantation owners, enthusiastically backed by the multi-talented and extremely wealthy Sir Joseph Banks, who had been much impressed with the description of breadfruit given by the buccaneer-explorer, William Dampier:

'When the fruit is ripe, it is yellow and soft, and the taste is sweet and pleasant'. When picked green and baked in the oven, a transformation took place and the inside became 'soft, tender and white as a pennyloaf'. There was neither 'seed nor stone' inside, and all was 'of a pure substance, like bread'.

England, represented by the merchants, by Banks, and by George III himself, saw breadfruit as a source of cheap food for slaves who, inconveniently, required to be fed. The produce of a couple of trees, it was thought,

Far left: Captain Bligh – John Smart
Left: Breadfruit – George Tobin
Above: No authenticated likeness of Fletcher Christian exists. This version, by Learmonth, from Richard Hough's 'Captain Bligh and Mr. Christian', is based on contemporary accounts.
Below: H.M.S. 'Bounty'

H.M.S. BOUNTY 1787-1789

could feed a slave for a whole year at a cost of nothing at all.

To offer in exchange for this treasure trove of 1000 plants, the *Bounty* carried a bizarre collection of chisels, knives, hatchets, hand-saws, gimlets, files, rasps, iron bars, nails, looking glasses, shirts and beads. The total value of these trading goods was £125 6s. 4d.

Ironically, breadfruit, the cause of so much enterprise and agony, was badly overrated. When it was finally introduced to the plantations, the slaves refused to eat it, either baked or *au naturel*.

But Sir Joseph was not to know that, and no expense was spared to equip the *Bounty* as a floating greenhouse. The purchase price of the vessel was £1950; the cost of her outfitting, £4456.

The *Bounty* was just 91 feet long. The arrangements made to carry her breadfruit plants were wonderful. The arrangements made for her crew were terrible. She had virtually no superstructure. All living would be conducted below decks in near darkness and claustrophobic cramp. The cabins provided for the majority of the men measured six feet by five. Such conditions would call for strong discipline and *Bounty*'s owners were confident that they had the right man for the job in Lieutenant (not yet Captain) William Bligh.

Bligh's origins were not as lowly as have sometimes been portrayed. In those unremittingly class-conscious days, his family would have been described as 'good yeoman stock'. He grew up in Plymouth, a city pervaded by the sea, where at the age of 13, he could quite

Below: Plans of the launch in which Bligh made his famous journey – National Maritime Museum, England. Bligh was unhappy with the size of the launch and insisted that it be replaced with a larger one – a decision which may have been motivated by an uncanny premonition.
Below right: Plans for refurbishments to the 'Bounty' to accommodate breadfruit plants – National Maritime Museum, England

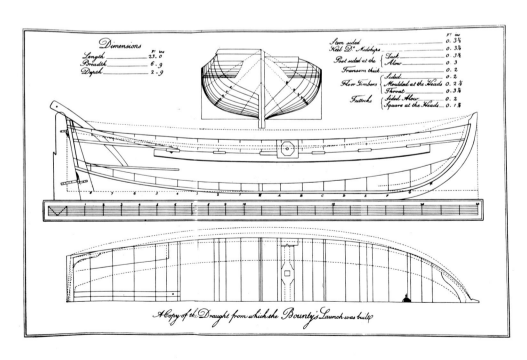

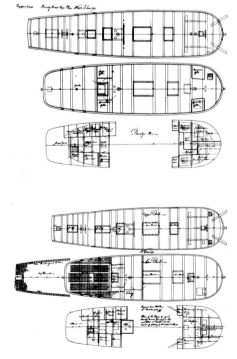

possibly have stood on the Sound with his father to see the departure of Captain Cook on the first of his three Pacific voyages. His father worked in Plymouth as a customs officer, a job which put him in touch with people of some influence with the Admiralty, and it was doubtless due to parental lobbying that Bligh was able to be 'registered' at the age of seven and to go to sea with certain privileges at the age of 15, on H.M.S. *Hunter*, a ten-gun sloop-of-war. Though this route into maritime service enabled Bligh to escape the depravities of serving on the lower deck, it was no soft touch. Sir John Barrow, who later wrote the first account of the mutiny to come, considered it Bligh's misfortune 'not to have been educated in the cockpit of a man-of-war, among young gentlemen, which is to the navy what a public

school is to those who move in civil society'.

But William Bligh survived. His naval record was distinguished, to say the least. He made a most favourable impression on the commander of the *Hunter*, saw action against the Carib Indians in the warship *Crescent* and by the time he was 20 was a fully-fledged midshipman serving on the *Ranger*, a warship engaged in hunting for smugglers in the Irish Sea. *Ranger* was based at Douglas, on the Isle of Man, and it was here, in the traditional stronghold of the Christians, that he met his wife-to-be, Betsy.

Betsy's relations were rich and influential. Her father, Richard Betham, counted amongst his friends the philosopher, David Hume, and the economist, Adam Smith. Her grandfather, Dr. Neil Campbell, was Chaplain to the King

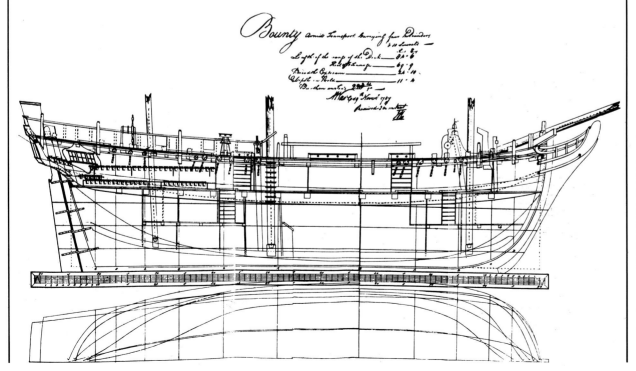

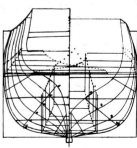

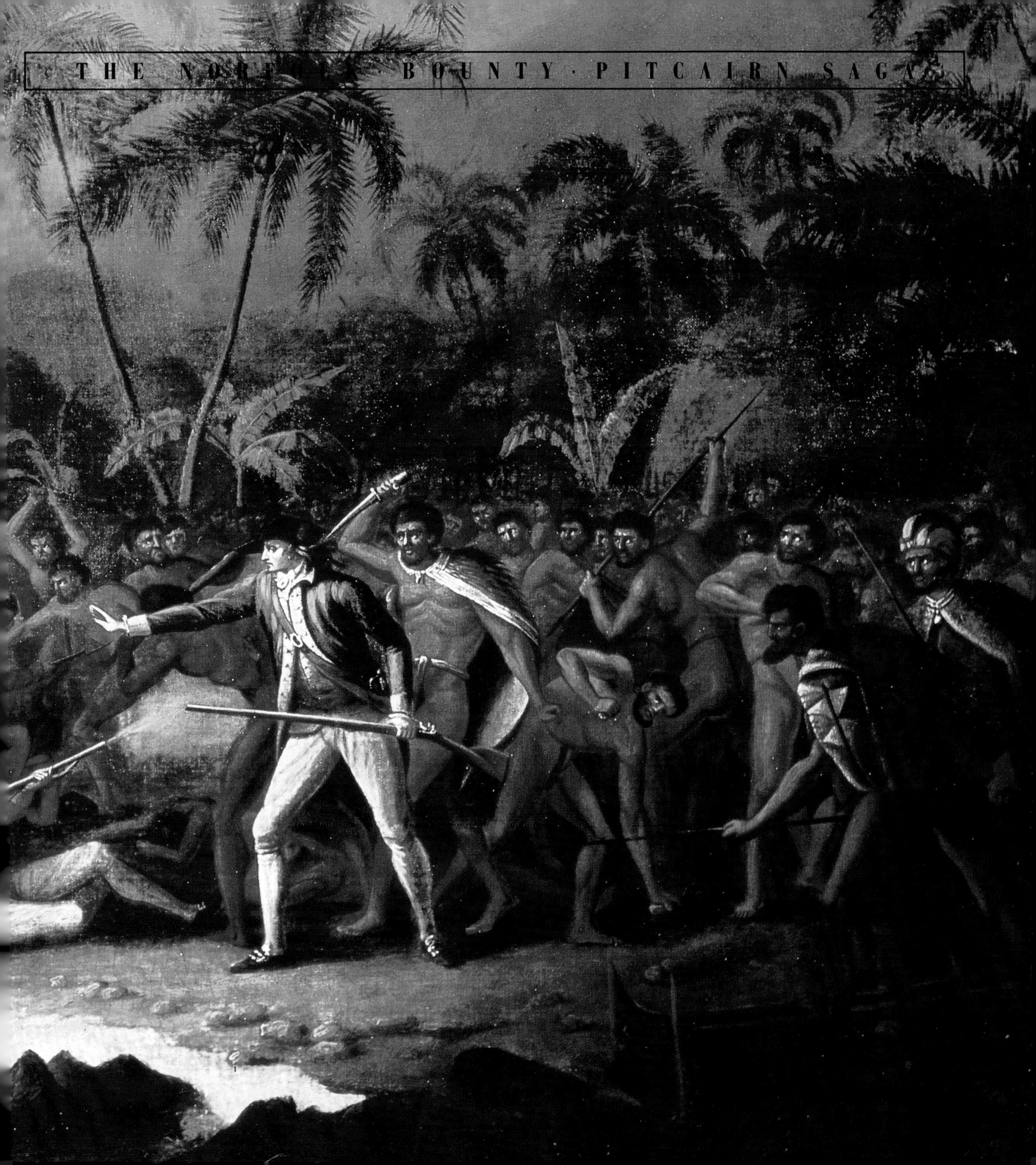

Previous spread: 'Death of Cook' –
John Webber

and Principal of Glasgow University. Her uncle, Duncan Campbell, was the owner of ships and plantations.

Bligh and Betsy were in no doubt of their intentions to marry but the happy day had to wait a further five years as Bligh now met with a singular honour: he caught the eye of the most eminent explorer of the day, Captain James Cook.

At the age of 21, he was appointed Master on the *Resolution*, the flagship on Cook's third voyage, the principal object of which was to seek a North-west Passage from the Pacific to the Atlantic.

During the two and a half years that Bligh sailed with the great captain, in unknown regions of the Pacific and amidst the ice-packs above Alaska, he matched Cook in many respects and even bettered him in some. He was a highly qualified nautical astronomer, an excellent navigator and hydrographer, a dedicated scientific researcher and a splendid cartographer. His drawings of plants, animals and birds were not only accurate but demonstrated a fine, sensitive line.

Captain Cook signified his respect for his young Master by naming one of the islands of the Kerguelen archipelago *Bligh's Cap*. But Bligh's relations with his shipmates were far from cordial. They remembered him as a man whose aesthetic face and 'woman's complexion' were counterpointed with piercing blue eyes, thin lips and a countenance that 'ever reflected a blazing ambition'. His powers of observation were remarkable but this made him all the more resentful of the inaccuracies which he found in all reports but his own and Cook's. His criticism of all around him was prolific, his praise miserly. At the least hint of criticism of himself,

Bligh was said to seethe with spite.

The tragic circumstances of Captain Cook's death at Kealakekua Bay were reported to the Admiralty in an account which Bligh believed was unduly influenced by Second Lieutenant King. The report suggested that the cause of the natives' rage was the killing of a Hawaiian chief by a shot fired from a boat under Bligh's command. It went on to praise the gallantry of Lieutenant Molesworth Phillips.

This Bligh described as 'an infamous lie'. There was not 'a spark of Courage or Conduct shown in the whole busyness', he wrote. 'The Marines fired and ran which occasioned all that followed, for had they fixed their bayonets & not have run, so frightened as they were, they might have drove all before them.'

As for Molesworth Phillips, 'this person, who never was of any real service the whole voyage, or did anything but eat and Sleep, was a great Crony of C. King's, and he has taken care not to forget, altho' it is very laughable to those who knew the Characters'.

By the time Bligh was appointed to command the *Bounty*, the roots of his character were set. His maritime skills, his courage and probity were undoubted, but along with those qualities went a pathological conviction of his own superiority. This was exacerbated by a foul temper and an excruciatingly cruel tongue.

For nearly two centuries it has suited the cause of drama to portray Bligh as a callous disciplinarian. In fact, he was not a harsh man by the standards of that day. In a period when, on Norfolk Island, sentences of up to 300 lashes were common, Bligh rarely ordered more than a dozen or two. Tales of his having denied water to his crew in favour of the breadfruit plants, and of three men having died as a result, are untrue.

As for his having keel-hauled a man, as was portrayed in a famous film, this is fiction.

He had a fanatical regard for the health of his crew, one instance of which was his employment on the *Bounty* of a fiddler (whose near-blindness did not impair his playing) to ensure that the men received exercise through dancing.

But to his own few shortcomings, Bligh was blind. On the second breadfruit journey, his relative and First Lieutenant, Francis Bond, wrote a letter to his brother which bears damning witness.

Yes, Tom, our relation has the credit of being a tyrant in his last expedition, where his misfortunes and good fortune elevated him to a situation he is incapable of supporting with decent modesty. The very high opinion he has of himself makes him hold everyone of our profession with contempt, perhaps envy: nay the Navy is but (a) sphere for fops and lubbers to swarm in, without one gem to vie in brilliancy with himself.

I don't mean to depreciate his extensive knowledge as a seaman and nautical astronomer, but condemn that want of modesty in self estimation.

To be less prolix I will inform you he has treated me (nay all on board) with the insolence and arrogance of a 'Jacobs': and notwithstanding his passion is partly to be attributed to a nervous fever with which he has been attacked most of the voyage, the chief part of his conduct must have arisen from the fury of an ungovernable temper.

Soon after leaving England I wished to receive instruction from this imperious master, until I found he publickly exposed any deficiency on my part in the Nautical Art, etc. A series of this conduct determined me to trust myself, which I hope will in some measure repay me for the trouble of this disagreeable voyage – in itself pleasant, but made otherwise by being worried at every opportunity.

His maxims are of the nature that at once pronounce him an enemy to the lovers of Natural Philosophy; for to make use of his own words, 'No person can do the duty of a 1st lieut who does no more than write the day's work of his publick journal'. This is so inimical to the sentiments I always hope to retain, that I find the utmost difficulty in keeping on tolerable terms with him.

. . . Every dogma of power and consequence has been taken from the Lieutenants, to establish, as he thinks, his own reputation – what imbecility for a post Capn!

. . . Every officer who has nautical information, a knowledge of natural history, a taste for drawing, or any thing to constitute him proper for circumnavigating, becomes odious; for great as he is in his own good opinion, he must have entertained fears some of the ship's company meant to submit a spurious Narrative to the judgement and perusal of the publick.

. . . The 2nd August we left England and had pleasant w(eather) to Teneriffa, where Captain B. was taken very ill and from particular traits in his conduct (I) believe he was insane at times.

Recently it has become fashionable to whitewash the fatal flaws in Bligh's nature, but history bears witness to his constant treatment of his subordinates as knaves and fools.

The young man who was to serve under William Bligh as Master's Mate was the product of a rich and powerful dynasty. Fletcher Christian's birthplace, Moorland Close, in

Above: This plaque and other records in the Parish Church of St. Peter, Onchan, Isle of Man, where Bligh was married, testify to the regular attendance of the Heywood family. It is likely that they attended the wedding. This acquaintanceship did not prevent Bligh from attempting to have Peter Heywood, only 16 at the time of the 'Bounty' mutiny, hanged.

Cumbria, was described by the locals as having 'dog kennels better than most people's houses'. His father was brought up in the stupendous 42 bedroom manor of Ewanrigg in Cumberland, and before that the Christian family had been prominent on the Isle of Man for probably a thousand years, ever since the Vikings conquered it.

The line goes back to the Norse, Gillocrist, thence to McCrystyn. John McCrystyn was Deemster† in 1408 and, from then until 1693, eight McCrystyns in succession held the title.

The family continued to be noble and affluent when they extended their power and domicile to Cumbria, whilst still swaying Manx politics through the Tynwald.‡ This famous open-air parliament, the world's oldest with an unbroken tradition, was conducted on Tynwald Hill, which was physically owned by the Christian family for centuries.

In 1768, when Fletcher Christian was just four years old, his father died. Christian did his schooling in nearby Cockermouth where his

school-mates included the poets Isaac Wilkinson and William Wordsworth. Later in his schooling Wordsworth had, as his master, Fletcher's older brother, Edward. Wordsworth was a frequent visitor at the Christian house and Coleridge was also a friend of the family. Young Fletcher was constantly surrounded with people of romantic vision and he appears to have been something of a dreamy child though cheerful and active.

A legend which must have greatly influenced him was that of his great-great-grandfather, known as Brown William (in Norse, 'Illiam Dhone'), an alleged mutineer against British rule. Executed for treason in 1663 at a place called Hango Hill, he was absolved from this charge rather too late and

posthumously pardoned. His confiscated property was restored to his wife and sons and 'Illiam Dhone' became a martyr-hero of the Manx.

Fletcher Christian grew up in a family which, whilst highly privileged, set great store by democratic principles. He would have been indoctrinated with the ritual of the reading of the new laws each Midsummer Day by the First Deemster of the Isle of Man, still read to this day so 'that no man can plead ignorance of them and no official secretly impose his rule'.

† *Deemster – 'he who pronounces the dooms' – the Chief Deemster was the highest of all the Manxmen.*
‡ *Scan.:'Thing' = assembly; 'Vollr' = field; thus, 'place of the assembly'.*

Opposite, far left: Fletcher Christian
Opposite, left: Christian's birthplace, Moorland Close – today sadly fallen into decay
Above: William Wordsworth – B. Holl
Below left: 'Laws of the Tynwald, 1795' – Manx Museum. Composed of soil from each of the original Manx kingdoms, Tynwald Hill still plays a central role in the world's oldest parliament which celebrated its millenium in 1979.

The Deemster's Oath reflects the Manxmen's sea-infused nature. It concludes: 'I do swear that I will, without respect of favour or friendship, love or gain, consanguinity or affinity, envy or malice, execute the laws . . . betwixt party and party, as indifferently as the herring backbone doth lie in the midst of the fish'.

The Christian clan was at its zenith in the late eighteenth century, its sons being prepared for the highest offices of the Law, the Church, the Cabinet and the Universities. However, two of Fletcher's elder brothers, to further their careers, borrowed with such astonishing recklessness that they bankrupted the immediate family. Perhaps this disaster strengthened his conviction that privilege should never be abused. In any event it apparently gave him a distaste for commerce. In his late teens, accounts of the voyages of Wallis, Carteret, Byron and Cook, and the exploits of Admirals Hood, Howe and Rodney began to work their magic. He elected for a career in the Navy at the relatively ancient age of 18.

He spent two years as a midshipman on the *Eurydice*, liked the life, did well at it, and decided that a voyage under a master whom the illustrious James Cook had trained would be an invaluable experience. Bligh initially refused the request from Christian's parents, claiming that he had a full complement, at which Christian wrote back personally:

Wages are no object: I only wish to learn my profession, and if you would permit me to mess with the gentlemen, I will readily enter your ship as a foremaster, until there be a vacancy among the officers.

He made two voyages to the West Indies with Bligh on the *Britannia*, first as a gunner, then as a second mate. Gradually he earned Bligh's respect and then, quite rapidly, a strong affection grew between the two men.

When Christian signed on board the *Bounty*, he had grown into a striking figure, tall for his day at 5′9″, decidedly handsome, and muscular. His brother Charles wrote: 'He bared his arm and I was amazed at its brawniness. "This", says he, "has been acquired by hard labour".'

His fellow seamen swore that Fletcher was capable of making a standing jump from one barrel directly into another. Bligh later described him in his diary, with what degree of accuracy we do not know, as 'slightly bow-legged and inclined to sweat profusely'.

A fourth son, Christian appears to have exhibited characteristics more typical of an only child. Usually cheerful and exhilarating company, he was subject to moods of black brooding. These were short-lived but doubly disturbing to his friends because of their startling contrast with his normally ebullient nature. In his periods ashore, he had the reputation of being a lady-killer: women adored him, perhaps because of the thread of vulnerability which ran parallel with his self-confidence.

Like Bligh, Christian was convinced of his right to the respect of others. Bligh had his impeccable record as a navigator and scientist; Christian had a heritage of twenty-five generations of unbroken aristocracy. The Isle of Man may not have been as powerful in its day as were Egypt or Italy in theirs, but as a one-family dynasty, the Christians were unmatched by the Pharaohs or the Medici.

Shortly before the *Bounty* sailed, Fletcher visited his brother Charles who, it has recently been discovered†, had been involved in a mutiny. Had Charles been serving in the Royal Navy instead of the Merchant Navy, he would have been hanged from the yard-arm. In the event, he was suspended from service with the East India Company for two years. The Commander of the ship, Captain Rogers, may have been a strong contributor to the mutiny as he was fined the very substantial sum of five hundred pounds and suspended from trading.‡

The conversation the two brothers had that night must surely have included speculation on the degree of provocation which would justify mutiny. Later, in his autobiography, Charles issued the warning he may well have given Fletcher that night:

The Precepts and Doctrine of our Religious inculcate the Forgiveness of Injuries, but when men are cooped up for a long time in the Interior of a Ship, there oft prevails such a jarring Discordancy of Tempers and Conduct that it is enough on many Occasions, by repeated Acts of Irritation, to change the Disposition of a Lamb into that of an Animal fierce and resentful.

When, after many frustrating delays, the *Bounty* finally sailed from Spithead, two days before Christmas, she carried a crew of 45 hand-picked seamen. None of them were press-ganged: this was probably the first British armed ship to sail with an all-volunteer crew. Perhaps that was a mistake.

† *By Glynn Christian*
‡ *Archives of the East India Office, Whitehall (5/9/1787)*

Left: The Christian coat-of-arms – from a stained glass window, Isle of Man
Top: The Christian crest: a unicorn's head – 'Fairbairn's Crests'
Above: The Isle of Man, stronghold of the Christians for five centuries

CHAPTER 3

Paradise Found

The *Bounty* had a harrowing trip. For three dreadful weeks she tried to beat her way around Cape Horn. Three times she actually rounded its tip, only to be bludgeoned back again. Bligh finally reversed course, headed for the Cape of Good Hope, rounded Van Diemen's Land and pushed on up to Tahiti.

There, in Matavai Bay, the men of the *Bounty* were greeted with the most astonishing goodwill by the natives, to whom pale skin denoted royalty.

Thousands of canoes turned out to welcome them, including one which was far longer than the *Bounty* herself. The women, debarred by their religion from boarding canoes, swam out to the ship in their hundreds, their tapa-bark robes dissolving in the water.

After ten months at sea, sailing 27,000 miles, the impact of this overwhelming hospitality can only be imagined. To men whose remembrances of their homeland were

primarily of filthy harbours and bleak moors, here were emerald lagoons and golden sands back-dropped by stupendous peaks shrouded in gossamer haze. And in place of the poxy harlots of Portsmouth, here were beckoning the voluptuous, raven-haired daughters of Polynesia.

The climate, the sunsets, the total ambience of the island made the senses swoon. And the luscious, abundant food went far beyond their experience, indeed beyond their wildest imaginings.

For most of their lives at sea, these men existed on a staple diet of 'Ship's Biscuit'. It was made from pea flour and bone dust. This bone dust, it was said, came from the charnel houses. The biscuit could not be bitten through until old, and by then it was infested with weevils and maggots. Relief from this came in the form of salted beef which, following months or years of

Far left: 'Poedooa, Princess of Otaheite' – John Webber. Nan Kivell Collection, National Library of Australia
Left: 'Creek in Matavai Bay, Otaheite' – R. Batty
Above: Tahitian girl – sketch by Smyth of H.M.S. 'Blossom'
Below: 'Black-eyed Sue and Sweet Poll of Plymouth taking leave of their lovers who are going to Botany Bay' – Laurie and Whittle, 1794

Previous spread: 'A View of Karakakooa Bay in Ohwyee' – John Webber, 1781/4
Right: 'A dance in Otaheite' – John Webber

being shrunk in salt, was so hard that sailors carved mementoes from it. One man in every seven was lost through illness. Though the *Bounty*'s fare, thanks to Bligh's dedication to the health of his crews, was more edible than the regular Royal Navy victuals, it was still, by our standards, vile. But here was fresh, real meat, suckling pig, exquisitely textured fish, and exotic fruits in luxurious abundance. These delights were eagerly pressed upon them, together with garlands of flowers and, most enticing of all, women.

It was for good reason that the French explorer, Bougainville, two decades earlier, had named the island *Nouvel-Cythére* ('New Cythera') after the Greek Island near which

Aphrodite, the Goddess of Love, had been born out of the sea.†

His naturalist, Philibert Commerson, wrote that the Tahitians knew 'no other god but love; every day is consecrated to it, the whole island is its temple, all the women are its idols, all the men its worshippers'. The mating of the sexes was 'an act of religion', joyfully performed in public. Commerson was convinced that this was 'the condition of natural man, born essentially good, free of all preconception, and following without diffidence or remorse the sweet impulse of an instinct always sound, because it has not yet degenerated into reason'.

In Bligh's previous visit to the island, as Master of Cook's *Resolution*, he purported to be

Left: 'Transplanting of the breadfruit trees' – Thomas Crosse, 1782. Nan Kivell Collection, National Library of Australia. The voluminous 'togas' depicted in these illustrations appear ridiculously romanticised but the Tahitians actually did wear such garments. To visiting Europeans, the Tahitian culture appeared to have mystic links with the Golden Age of Greece. One explorer ran a tape over a chief and swore that his measurements were identical with those of the Apollo Belvedere!

shocked at the morals of the residents, but Midshipman George Gilbert described the Tahitian women as 'the most beautiful we have met in the South Seas . . . full of gaiety and good humour'.

'Their songs and dances, which are very frequent, appear exceeding lascivious in the eyes of a European', he wrote, but noted that 'the custom of the country . . . seemingly permits them to pursue the natural impulse of their passions'. He continued: 'These Islanders beyond a doubt live in the most perfect state of freedom, friendship and happiness of any people in the world; and still enjoy all the pleasures of the Golden Age which is now nowhere else to be found'.

On his visit with Cook, Sir Joseph Banks was similarly enraptured: 'I have nowhere seen such Elegant women as those of Otaheite', he wrote, 'such as might even defy the Chizzel of a Phidias or the Pencil of an Apelles'. As for the suitability of their bodies and willing souls for erotic pursuits, they were 'modeld into the utmost perfection for that soft science'. To the *Bounty*'s crew, the concept of Free Love was as welcome as it was alien to their upbringing and they adopted it with instant enthusiasm.

Bligh did not deny his men these earthly

† *Bougainville believed he had discovered Tahiti. In fact, he had been beaten to the punch by the Englishman, Wallis, a year earlier.*

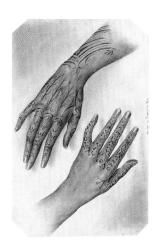

comforts but swiftly set them about the task of gathering the breadfruit plants which he was to transport to the Caribbean slave plantations. It has been claimed that the reason for Bligh's protracted stay in Tahiti was because he needed to await the fertility season of the breadfruit plants. It has subsequently been demonstrated that they were ready to be gathered and that this took no longer than three weeks. They stayed for another twenty.

Bligh was far too conscientious and ambitious to have taken this decision without good reason, and probably fear of impossible

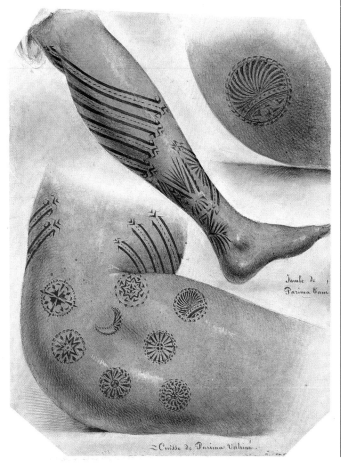

weather around the Horn was that reason, but it is apparent that, in his fashion, he enjoyed the stay. It was not long before the work ethic with which he had so assiduously indoctrinated his crew was eroded by the sensual environment which enveloped them all.

Soused in the life-style which was subsequently to enchant thousands of Europeans, including Gauguin, Herman Melville and R.L. Stevenson, the crew became daily more willing to identify themselves with the customs of their hosts, to such an extent that several of them, including Fletcher Christian, underwent agonising buttock tattoos.

Joseph Banks himself had made tattooing to some extent acceptable by acquiring a small hand decoration during the course of his voyage with Cook. But the full buttock tattoo was something else. It involved many hours of stoic resolution as thousands of sharp blows were struck with a bone instrument dipped in lampblack, each blow drawing blood.

When we visualise a dapper Fletcher Christian in his full midshipman's uniform, we should remember that beneath those vestments he wore symbols of his commitment to a most un-English life-style.

For four months the men did little else but join the Tahitians in an endless round of games. Popular were stilt-walking, kite-flying, spear-throwing and wrestling. More popular still was simply gorging themselves at gargantuan feasts and being entertained by dancing on a scale for which their British upbringing had little prepared them. But the pastime they applied themselves to most rapturously was the Art of Love, Tahitian style.

Christian, called 'Titreano' by the eager Tahitian 'wahines', shared many a bed with

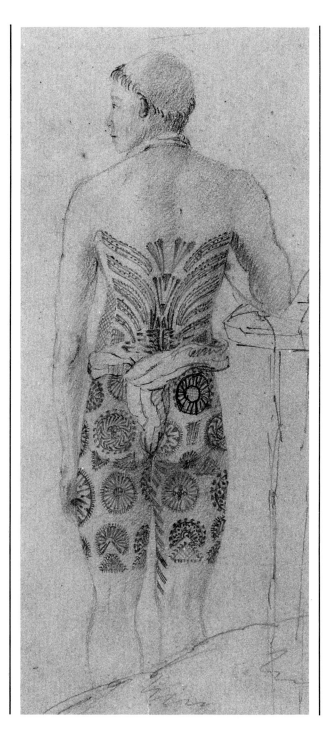

them until he chose to form a steady alliance with the chieftain's daughter, Mauatua (also called Mi'Mitti), whom he renamed Isobella.†

For centuries, it had been mandatory for Christian's aristocratic Manx forbears to choose an heiress as a partner. In this new world, Fletcher followed tradition, but her gifts to him were to prove non-materialistic.

This tropical idyll came to an end on the 4th of April, 1789, when the *Bounty*, with a thousand breadfruit plants aboard, plus many gifts from the island chiefs to King George, finally set sail for the West Indies. Bligh's instructions required him to sail halfway around the known world, including another attempt to round Cape Horn, and even Bligh anticipated a fearful voyage.

A fearful voyage it proved to be, though not the one he had planned.

† *Some historians claim he married her and that Alexander Smith and Quintal were probably also married. Professor H.E. Maude, of the Australian National University, believes Christian married 'Isobella' on his first visit to Tahiti and has so informed the College of Arms.*

Next spread: 'Canoes of Otahytey' – George Tobin

Opposite, far left: Tahitian hand tattoos
Opposite, left: Tahitian tattoos on buttocks, leg and thigh
Left: Tahitian tattoos on back, buttocks and thighs
Below: Tahitian tattooist at work – from a sketch in the diary of Smyth of H.M.S. 'Blossom'

CHAPTER 4

Prologue to Mutiny

Having let discipline erode almost completely on Tahiti, Bligh made an instant transition, when the boat sailed, into a taskmaster impossible to please. Not with the cat-o'-nine-tails, but with that uniquely vicious tongue, he lashed unremittingly at crew and officers alike.

Three weeks out from Tahiti, the *Bounty* anchored off Nomuka, in the so-called Friendly Islands. The natives were in a far-from-friendly mood and Christian, who was in command of the landing party, informed Bligh of their threatening demeanour. For this, Bligh 'damned him for a cowardly rascal', asking if he were afraid of a 'set of Naked Savages while he had Arms'.

Bligh's sudden accusation came like a bludgeon blow to Christian. In his previous voyages with Bligh, they were reported to have had occasional arguments, notably in Cape Town and in Adventure Bay, Van Diemen's Land, over a money loan that Bligh had made to his protegé, but until that moment they appeared to have been more than tolerably good friends. Christian would have been aware that a rift had grown between them on Tahiti as a result of their very different appreciation of that enticing life-style. He could have been conscious of a mounting jealousy on Bligh's part. But nothing would have prepared him for scorching abuse in front of his fellow officers.

Christian replied, 'The arms are of no use while your orders prevent them being used'.

Work continued but, after further provocations by the natives, the party was lucky to escape with the loss of only a grapnel from the ship's dinghy. At this, Bligh fell into a totally unreasonable rage and, to the astonishment of the crew, ordered that five of the native chiefs should be kidnapped. One was released and told to report to his subjects that, as punishment for their theft of the grapnel, they would never see their other chiefs again. This resulted in the *Bounty* being pursued for miles by canoes filled with men and women weeping and mutilating themselves in a terrible and bloody manner, beating their heads with paddles and gashing their faces with sharks' teeth.

Far left: Fletcher Christian as depicted by Robert Dodd. Detail from 'Lieutenant Bligh leaving the Bounty' – National Maritime Museum, England
Above left: H.M. Armed Vessel 'Bounty' – National Maritime Museum, England
Below: 'A view of Anamooka' – John Webber

Bligh eventually released the chiefs but this irrational show of pique deeply disillusioned Christian. In humiliating the Tahitian chiefs, Bligh was spitting in the faces of those of the crew who had adopted Tahitian philosophies so whole-heartedly.

Certainly, the appeal of Tahiti to the crew was, to an enormous degree, sexual. But there was more. To Christian, a man of broader education and keener sensitivity than Bligh, Tahitian culture also had a philosophical appeal. What had brought Europeans to the Pacific was a thirst for knowledge, riches and power. The stunningly different culture they found there made many – Herman Melville and, later, R.L. Stevenson and Paul Gauguin among them – see things in a profoundly different light. Western values and motivations, unquestioned for generations, now appeared complex, cruel and crass.

Bligh, however, was intractable. Later that night, he found another opportunity to humiliate his officers. He announced that a pile of coconuts belonging to him had 'shrunk' overnight and subjected the crew to a vicious cross-examination. Christian, deeply hurt, asked, 'I hope you don't think me to be so mean as to steal yours?', to which Bligh replied, in front of the officers as well as the crew, 'Yes, you Hound, I do!' These words have been reported by eye-witnesses with such unanimity that we must assume they were actually used by Bligh. Crew members later admitted that Christian had helped himself to one solitary coconut. They had been bought at the rate of twenty for an iron nail.

It has been suggested in books and films that many of the officers were sympathetic to Bligh. Though the majority were under-standably unwilling to be actively involved in a mutiny, sympathy was not an emotion that could reasonably be expected of them in the aftermath of Bligh's vicious abuse of them from the moment of the *Bounty*'s sailing. In one of his more incredible utterances, he had threatened that 'only half the officers would survive the journey home as he would throw them overboard in the Endeavour Straits'. Scores of men who sailed with Bligh spoke with awe of his incredible facility in the art of insult. His obscenity literally took their breath away. Throughout his career, Bligh was obsessed with the conviction that he was inflicted with subordinates who were such incompetents or delinquents that no language was sufficiently vicious to do justice to their failings. And it was on his ex-friend, Christian, that he now turned the full force of his invective.

Perhaps pure jealousy was his motivation or perhaps he believed that Christian's popularity with the crew was a token that he was too soft on them at a time when Bligh was hell-bent on subduing them. In any event, as the ship's carpenter Purcell later testified, 'Bligh's constant bullying reduced Christian to tears'. Sobbing with mortification, Christian told Purcell that he was sure that if he did so much as to answer Bligh back he would be flogged. If that were to happen, he averred, 'it would be the death of us both, for I am sure I should take him in my arms and jump overboard with him'. To the boatswain, he claimed that he had been 'used like a dog'. On three separate occasions he told shipmates that he had 'been in Hell this fortnight past', and declared that he was 'determined to bear it no longer'.

Unbearably humiliating as Bligh's sarcasm must have been to a man of Christian's

Above: Tahitian tattoos on belly and legs

privileged background, it is unlikely that this alone would have driven him to such an irreversible step as mutiny were it not for the fact that as Hell was mounting Paradise was receding. And it was not purely a sensual loss – it appears highly probable that Christian's affection for Isobella was such that he had married her and – a point which has had little stress – that he had left her pregnant.†

Driven to something approaching what today we might call 'temporary insanity', he at first planned to desert ship and had put together a rough raft and a cache of provisions. During the fateful night which followed, he must have decided that this course was too unmanly, or, perhaps, too easy on his tormentor. He began to think about the unthinkable.

Those who would support him in a mutiny would not be the cream of the crew. There were two desperados, the fiery, red-headed Scot, Will McCoy, and the tough, stocky, fair-haired Cornishman, Matt Quintal, who could be counted upon to make trouble wherever it was to be had. There was the tall American, Isaac Martin, who had often been abused and recently flogged by Bligh and resented it. Charley Churchill, Master-at-Arms, was a likely prospect. He had deserted and been punished by flogging, confinement in irons and flogging again. Ned Young, the swarthy, part West Indian but well-educated nephew of a navy captain, was of a different mould. He was a good friend and had made certain private observations which verged on insurgency.

Christian was not too sure of Alexander Smith. He knew that Smith's real name was John Adams and that he had signed aboard the *Bounty* under an assumed name, but that was common practice. Though he was nicknamed

'Reckless Jack', he seemed a mild enough fellow. The important thing was that he was a great respecter of Christian‡ and no lover of Bligh. There were other likelies, the gunner's mate Mills and seamen Williams, Muspratt, Burkett and Ellison, and a few possibles like Brown, the botanist's assistant.

During the morning watch, within sight of the erupting Tofua volcano, Christian's smouldering sense of injustice turned into an unstoppable conviction that he must be 'rid of this man forever'.

ILE TOFOUA

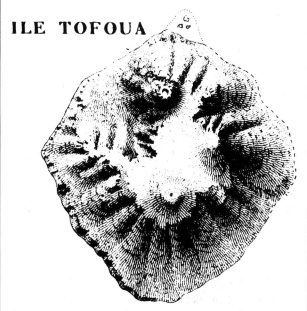

ILE KAA

Left and above: The volcanic island of Tofua and its satellite Kaa – from a sketch made during the journey of the French corvette 'L'Astrolobe'

† *Historians have traditionally assumed that Christian's son was born on Pitcairn but unless Thursday October lied about his age, which seems unlikely, he was actually born on the 'Bounty'. In 1808, he told Captain Folger he was 18 and to the captains of the 'Briton' and 'Targus' in 1814 he gave his age as 25. This would have put his birth year as 1789 and his birth place as the 'Bounty'. Conception would thus have been in Tahiti.*
‡ *Thirty years after Christian's death, John Adams still referred to him as 'Mr. Christian'.*

CHAPTER 5

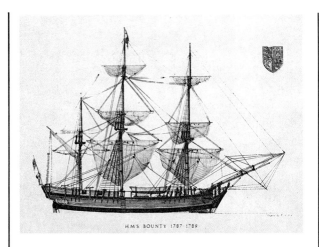

H.M.S BOUNTY 1787 1789

The Eruption

Once Christian had decided to fight rather than flee, he moved with unstoppable resolution.

Awakening the armourer, Coleman, he asked for the keys to the arms chest, saying he wanted to shoot a shark. He gathered several dissidents around the chest where, they later testified, 'his countenance turned to thunder'. No one will ever know for certain, but it appears very likely that until that moment not one of the crew, with the possible exception of Edward Young, had an inkling of Christian's intent to mutiny.

On Tuesday, 28th April, 1789, Bligh wrote in his journal:

...just before sunrise, Mr. Christian, Mate, Chas. Churchill, Ship's Corporal, John Mills, Gunner's Mate, and Thomas Birkett, Seaman, came into my cabin while I was asleep, and seizing me tyed my hands with a cord behind my back, and threatened me with instant death if I spoke or made the least noise.

I however called so loud as to alarm everyone,†but the Officers found themselves secured by Centinels at their Doors. There were four men in my cabin and three outside viz. Alexr. Smith, Jn. Sumner and Matw. Quintal. Mr. Christian had a Cutlass in his hand, the others had Musquets and Bayonets.

I was forced on Deck in my shirt, suffering great pain from the Violence with which they had tied my hands. I demanded the reason for such a violent act but I received no Answer but threats of instant death if I did not hold my tongue.

... I continued to endeavour to change the Tide of Affairs, when Christian changed the Cutlass he had in his hand for a Bayonet that was brought to him, and holding me with a Strong Grip to the cord that tied my hands, continued to threaten me with instant death if I did not be quiet.

The Villains around me had their pieces cocked and Bayonets fixed, and particular People were now Called upon to go in the Boat, and were hurried over the side, with these people I concluded of course I was to be set adrift.

I therefore, in making another effort to bring about a Change, expressed myself in such a manner as to be saluted with 'Blow his Brains out'.

Though a certain amount of abuse was obviously hurled at Bligh, it was one of the most bloodless coups in history, the chafing of Bligh's wrists being the closest approach to blood-letting in the entire incident.

Mental wounds, of course, were another matter, and Bligh had to endure the supreme

† *Bligh's shout was 'Murder!', over and over again.*

Far left: This sketch from H. K. Browne's version of the mutiny, depicting a villainous, portly Fletcher Christian armed with a musket and pistol, demonstrates that pro-Bligh sentiments are not new.
Left: H.M.S. 'Bounty'

who it now appears were certainly innocent. — With such deep laid plans of Villany and my mind free of any suspicions it is not wonderful I have been got the better of. But the possibility of such a Catastrophe, was ever the farthest from my thoughts. Christian was to have dined with me and supped the preceding evening, but he desired to be excused as he found himself unwell, about which I was concerned rather than suspecting his integrity and honor. —

It now remained with me what was best to be done, and I determined that after getting a Supply of Bread fruit and Water at Tofoa to sail for Amsterdam and there risk a solicitation to Poulehow to equip my Boat and grant a Supply so as to enable me to return towards Home. —

The exact quantity of Provisions I found they had got in the Boat was 150 lbs Bread 16 pieces of Pork, 6 Quarts of Rum. 6 Bottles of Wine with 28 Gallt of Water and four Empty Breakers. —

Wm Bligh

Above and far right: Facsimiles from Bligh's 'A Voyage to the South Sea...'
Right: Draft from which launch for the 'Bounty' was built

humiliation of being dragged trouserless on deck, the hasty cord which bound him catching his shirt in such a fashion that seaman Burkett was moved to try and readjust it to 'cover his shame'.

'As for Christian,' wrote Bligh in his *Narrative*, 'he seemed to be plodding (sic) instant destruction on himself and every one, for of all diabolical looking men he exceeded every discription'.

Bligh bravely continued to bluster until Christian gave him the final ultimatum:

Come, Captain Bligh, your Officers and Men are now in the Boat and you must go with them. If you attempt to make the slightest resistance, you will instantly be put to death.

The Narrative continues:

...forcing me before him, holding the Cord that wrapped my hands behind my back, and a Bayonet in the other, with a Tribe of Armed Ruffians about me I was forced over the side.

...When we came away, 'Huzzah for Otaheite' was frequently heard among the Mutineers.

One of the most persistent acts of character assassination perpetrated upon Christian down the years has been the avowal that he mercilessly set Bligh and the loyalists adrift on a trackless sea with little hope of survival.

In fact, Bligh was in sight of Tofua and made landing there that very night. Christian showed surprising – or foolish – generosity in presenting him with his own sextant which would enable Bligh to venture beyond Tofua for no one had a greater admiration for Bligh's navigational skills than Christian. He also provided the launch with 150 pounds of bread, 20 pounds of pork, 28 gallons of water, 5 quarts of rum, some wine, breadfruit and coconuts, and a few clothes. At the last moment, four cutlasses were thrown into the boat.

What Christian had no way of knowing, however, was that news of Bligh's treatment of the Nomukan chiefs had been conveyed to the Tofuans. As the Britishers were completing their gathering of provisions, they were showered with stones. The Quartermaster was killed and the others were lucky to be able to launch the boat. Pursued by the natives in their war canoes, they were saved by Bligh's resourceful action of throwing overboard clothes which the natives stopped to pick up.

Bligh decided to head for Timor. The Norfolk Island colony was thousands of miles closer but Bligh apparently decided that he could not take the risk of it having been successfully established. (Had he done so, Norfolk might eventually have seen descendants of the loyalists living alongside those of the mutineers!)

What was to follow was one of the most astonishing feats of navigation — and raw, unremitting courage — in the history of the sea.

If you can imagine yourself in a boat measuring 23 feet by 6 feet 9 inches, jam-packed with 18 desperate, starving men, with 7 inches of freeway (on one of the few calm days,

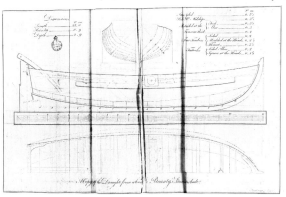

Remt. in the Bountys Launch. Wednesday 29th April 1789 at Tofoa

Happily the Afternoon kept Calm untill about 4 O'Clock, when we were so far to Windward that with a Moderate Easterly breeze which sprung up we were able to sail – it was neverthelefs dark when we got under Tofoa where I expected to land, but the shore proved to be so steep and Rocky that I was Obliged to give up all thoughts of it and keep the Boat under the Island with two Oars. for there was no landing   Having fixed on this mode of proceeding for the Night. I servd to every person two Gills of Grog, and each took his rest in proportion as they reflected on their unhappy Situation

In the Morning at dawn of day we set off along shore in search of landing, and about 10 O'Clock we discovered a Stoney Cove at the NW part of the Island where I dropt the Grapnel within 20 Yards of the Rocks. – A great deal of Surf run on the shore, but as I determined to encrease our Original Stock of provisions rather than diminish it, I sent out Mr. Samuel and some others who Climbed the Cliff to get into the Country to search for Supplies. – The rest of us remained at the Cove after discovering no way to get into the Country but that by which Mr. Samuel had proceeded. – I became happy to find the Spirits and life of my people were raised, and that our miserable Situation may be forever known to the World. I made an Observation of the Latitude which determines this Cove to lie in 19–41 S° on the N W side of Tofoa. – the Westermost of the Friendly Islands – The whole Coast we have seen is an entire precipice. – Towards Noon Mr. Samuel returned with a few Quarts of Water which he had found in the holes, of the that he had met with no Spring or any prospect of our Wants being relieved in that particular, and that he had only seen signs of the Island being inhabited. – As it was impofsible to say how much we might be in Want. I only ifsued a Morsel of Bread & a Glafs of Wine to each person for Dinner. ——

BOUNTY

let alone the others) and, day after day, rigorously writing up a detailed log in meticulous copperplate calligraphy, you can gain some insight into what manner of man was William Bligh.

He calculated that their provisions would normally have lasted for five days. He had the men agree that these should be spun out to fifty days.

They lived on one ounce of bread and a quarter of a pint of water per day, supplemented by ship's biscuit, an occasional mouthful of coconut, breadfruit or yam, the entrails of a

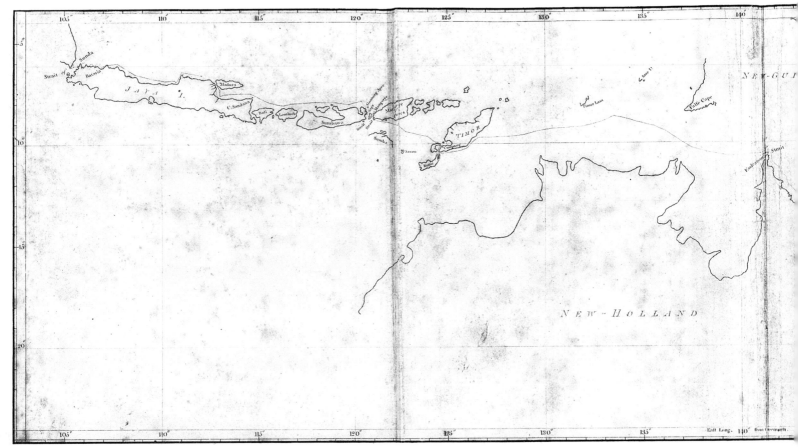

sea-bird, a thimbleful of its blood. And, for a treat, a teaspoonful of rum. For the dispensation of luxuries such as pork, Bligh rigged up some scales. He would cut up the meat and allot to each man a portion the weight of a bullet.

For an unbearable 21 of the 43 days, they were subjected to heavy and almost continuous rain, requiring almost constant bailing.

As they passed through the Great Barrier Reef, they were dissuaded from landing by natives on the shore, 'black, naked and heavily armed', but finally put ashore on an island in the

Previous spread: 'Lieutenant Bligh leaving the Bounty' – Robert Dodd, 1790. National Maritime Museum, England
Far left: 'Bligh's gourd, cup, bullet-weight, and book' – from the Rev. Thos. Boyle's 'Pitcairn – the island, the people and the pastor'
Below: 'Track of the Bounty's launch from Tofoa to Timor' – Bligh, 1789
Left: 'The open boat, with Bligh and his Companions' – R. Batty

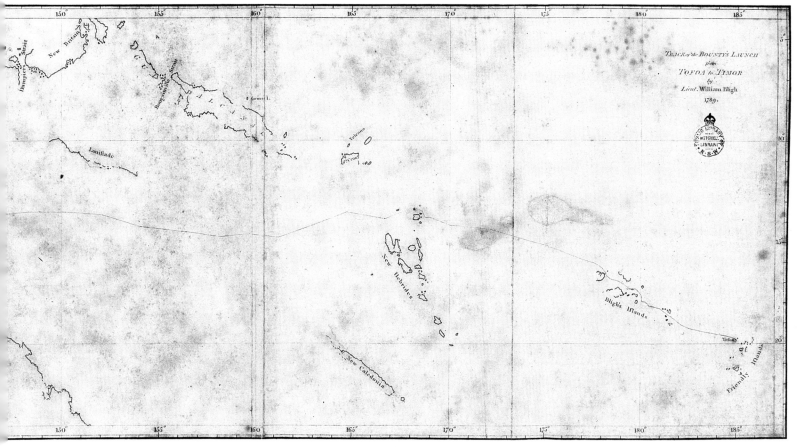

H	K	F	Courses	Winds	Rem.s Wednesday 6th May 1789 In the Bounty's Launch.
1	4		WNW	ENE	Very hazy Wr but fair
2	4				
3	4				
4	4				
5	3	4			Hauled the Wind saw two High Islands A NWbW 6 leagues and B
6	4		NWbW	NEbE	NWbW 8 leagues. – Fresh Breeze steered to Windward of the Northernmost
7	5	4			
8	5	4			Served two Cocoa Nuts for Supper –
9	5	4			
10	5	4			Bore up the Island B WbS 4 leagues.
11	5		NW		
12	4				
1	3	4			
2	4				
3	4				
4	4		WNW		
5	3	4			
6	5	4			The Isld B SSE 10 leagd. Saw 5 others a small one C SbW 5 leagues
7	3	4	NWbN	ENE	a little larger one D WbS ½ S 6 leagd a High Mountainous one E SW
8	4		NWbN		9 leagd. another middle doz F West 3 leagd and another G NEbE 7
9	2½		West		or 8 leagd. Steered between those two last. –
10	4				At 7h the Isld F bore true So and now proved to be two Islds with only
11	3	4			a Channel for Boats between them. – At 9h 35′ a Small Key H bore West
12	3				At 10h½ saw a large Isld I SW 8 leagd.
99					Fair Wr & hazy. The Key H SbW½ E 2 miles. The Isld E SbEbE 7 leagd. the
109					Isles F Et 5 leagd. An Isld K SbW½ W 5 leagd. Isld I SW to W. and discovered
2000					another large Isld L NbW 8 or 9 leagd dist.
			Mero All O Center	S16. 6	Served a half Gill of Cocoa Nut Milk and an oz of the Meat to each person for Dinner. –

Course	Dist	Latitude		Longitude
		Obsd.	DR	DR
N 50 W	84	17.. 17 S	17.. 10 S	179. 43 E

Whitsundays, where the discipline of near-death dissolved and they fell into factions which Bligh found difficult to resolve.

He wrote later:

I saw there was no carrying command with any certainty of Order but by power; for some had totally forgotten every degree of obedience.

...the carpenter (Purcell) began to be insolent to a high degree, and at last told me, with a mutinous aspect, he was as good a man as I was. I did not just now see where this was to end; I therefore determined to strike a final blow at it, and either to preserve my command or die in the attempt; and, taking hold of a cutlass, I ordered the rascal to take hold of another and to defend himself.

Though Fryer and others threatened trouble, the crisis passed.†

Once again on the open sea, Bligh continued to keep his meticulous diary, sketching, fixing his daily position, recording everything from the state of the current to the incidence of death-presaging torpor in his men.

After seven weeks of horror, they arrived at Timor, numbed with cold, tortured with constipation, exhausted with bailing and almost at famine point even though ample stores remained. They had reached Timor many days earlier than Bligh had calculated, having made the remarkable progress of almost ninety miles a day.

As dawn broke on June 14th, they were towed into Coupang harbour by a local hired with Rix dollars originally intended for the purchase of breadfruit plants. Their clothing reduced to rags, their bodies reduced to bones, their legs horribly swollen and their skin running with sores, the men were forced to remain in the boat whilst Bligh, with a near-manic regard for convention, raised a flag of distress and insisted on waiting until he had received formal permission to land.

Eighteen of the original 19 were still alive, the only exception being the Quartermaster who had been killed by the Tofuans on day 2. But at Coupang, debilitated by the journey and thus ready prey to malaria and other tropical diseases, six died.

† *If we could call this episode a mutiny, Bligh was involved in four during his lifetime. Sir John Barrow says that Purcell ended his days in a 'madhouse'.*

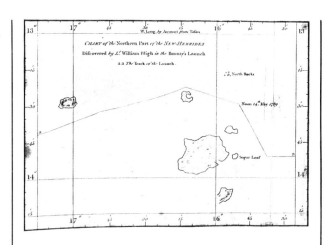

Far left: Page from Bligh's log
Below left: 'Lieut. Bligh and his crew of the ship Bounty hospitably received by the Governor of Timor' – Ashburn's 'History of England', 1779
Above left: One of Bligh's discoveries during the open boat journey
Above: Engraving of Captain Bligh after his ordeal

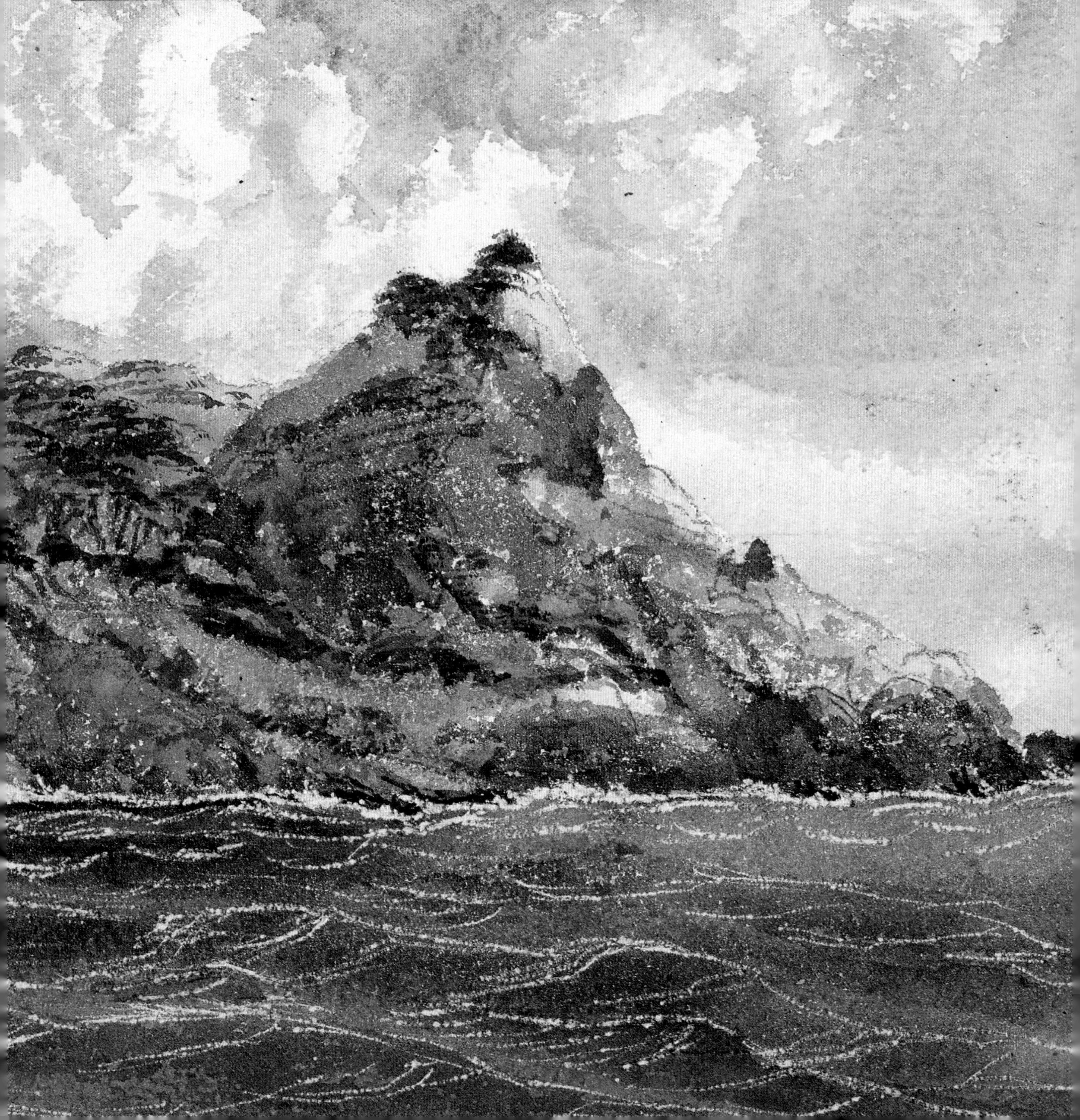

CHAPTER 6

The 8000 Mile Quest

Books and films have suggested that Christian was hell-bent on returning to Tahiti. Though he must certainly have been tempted to return to pick up Isobella, he calculated that to go back immediately would be to risk finding himself stuck with a crew who refused to leave. But Bligh was convinced that the motivation for the mutiny was the allurement of the Tahitian life-style and believed that the 'pirates' would lose no time in returning there.

'What a temptation it is to such wretches,' he wrote in his diary, 'when they find it in their power, however illegally it can be got at, to fix themselves in the midst of plenty on the finest island in the world where they need not labour and where allurements of dissipation are more than equal to anything to be conceived'.

Christian, however, rejected the demands of many of his crew. He scoured Bligh's books of navigation where he learned of the discovery by Captain Cook in the previous year of an island called Toobouai, 350 miles south of Tahiti, exactly on the Tropic of Capricorn. He headed directly there.

As Cook had not landed on the island he was not able to report on the disposition of the inhabitants. As a precaution, Christian, observing that 'nothing has more effect on the mind of the Indians than a uniformity of dress', ordered that some spare sails be cut up and made into uniforms for the common seamen, who normally wore only working clothes. His own officer's outfit was used to provide edging.

Arriving at Toobouai on the 25th of May, he found it to have a topography strangely reminiscent of the Isle of Man but had little time to reflect on this as he found the natives extremely bellicose. Decked in war-paint, they flocked around the *Bounty* in scores of war-canoes, blowing fiercely on conch shells.

Some of the canoes contained women playing the role of sirens with the design of enticing the *Bounty* close enough to allow a boarding.

Far left: The Peak, Pitcairn
Left: Pitcairn, sketched by Smyth (of H.M.S. 'Blossom') from seven miles offshore
Below: Toobouai Island — from Philip Wilson's 'A New, Complete and Universal Collection of Authentic and Entertaining Voyages and Travels to All Parts of the World'

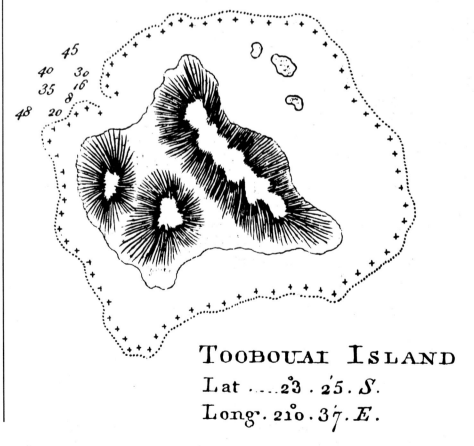

TOOBOUAI ISLAND
Lat .... 23°. 25. S.
Long. 210°. 37. E.

par Tasman

I. Woodle   I. Hopper
I. Henderville   I. Byron

I.ᵉˢ Baxos   Les Anachoretes   Mahia
La Boudeuse   l'Amirauté   I. Oregeou
Les Cocos   S.ᵗ Paul   Hanovre
I. de la Madeleine   Dukde Byr.   N.lle Irla
Vokan   Vokan   C. Anna
Nicolas   C.ᵉ Stephen   I. S.ᵗ Jean
Passage   I. Rooby

Terre Papoux

C. du R. Guillaume   de Dampier   I. Long
Guad-al-Canal   I. Rook
Brye Bay
l'Endeavour   Cul de de l'Orangerie   Louisiade
Golfe de la Louisiade   Oues.ᵗ C. de la Delivrance
York   Le Labyrinthe
Canal de la Providence   Passage de Bligh

Détroit de Bougainville   I. Alexandre   Choiseul déc.ᵗ par M. de Bougainville

I. Gower ou Inattendue   I. Carteret   I. Simson
A. Indi.   M. du Contrariétés   Les 3 Sœurs
B. Homme   Volcan   I. de l'Hirondelle
C. Marsh   C. Hunter   Swallow ou Koppel
C. Honslow   I. de la Reine Charlotte
C. Philipp   C. Sidney   I. How

ARCHIPEL.

I.ᵈᵘ du Lezard   I. de Direction de Cook   C. Flattery   C. Bedford
I. Hope   B. de la Trinité
Rockingham   Revue par M. de Bougainville
C. Tribulation   C. Grafton   M.ᵗ Double
Rockingham   M. Hillock ou du Mondrain
C. Sandwich   I. Palmes   Cleveland   Bowen
I. Holborn   Gloucester
M. Upstar   B. Edgecumbe

Nouvelle Galles Meridionalle

I.ᵉ Cumberland
I.ᵉ Northumberland
C. Palmerston   Townsend
B. d'Ialets   B. Keppel
C. Capricorne
C. Nord
I. Sud
I. Hervey
C. Sandy   P.ᵗᵉ Indienne
B. Large   P.ᵗ Double   de la Verrerie
Les Verrières   C. Morton   P.ᵗ Lockent
M.ᵗ Warning   P.ᵗ Danger
C. Byron
Les 3 Frères
I.ᵉ Solitaires
C. Smoakey, ou de la Fumée
I. du Lord Howe

nommé par M. Aurore de Bougainville
Terre du S.ᵗ Esprit
Passage de   I. de la Pentecôte   I. Ambrim
I. Mallicolo   I. Paoom   I. Apps   I. Shepherds
DᵉˢI. du Monuments   I. des Collines   I. Montagu
LES GRAN.ᵈᵉˢ   I. Sandwich   CYCLADES
I. Eromango   Cook
et par   I. Immer
I. Terraname ou Erronan
I. Sabloneuse   I. de l'Observatoire
I. Balabea   C. Collnet
NOUV.   I. Enalum ou Anatum   LES   HEBRIDES
LES   Nouv.lle   Caledonie
C. du Gouvernement
C. de la R.ᵉ Charlotte
Pr.ᵉⁿ du P.ᵗ de Galles   Botanique   I. Mathews
I. des Pins

I. Horn
I. du P.ᶜᵉ Guillaume, ou bas fonds d'Heemskerk
I. de Bligh ou Fee͏ée
I. de la Tortue

I. de Wall la belle
I. de l'Esp ou l'Esp
I. de l'Esperance
I. Koppel ou ...
... Traitres
Isles d
I. Toofoa
I. Rotterdam ou Annamooka
I. Tongataboo ou Amsterdam

I. de Middleton déc.ᵗ par Shortland en Juillet 1788
Banc de Middleton

I. Norfolk

I. Mᶜawley Curtis déc.ᵗ par M. Watz le 31 May 1788

C. Hawke   Port Stephens
Les 3 Pointes   Port Jackson
Botany Bay   Banks
I.e Colombier   C. Solander
C. Gr.ᵈ Nez
B. Batman   I.ᵉ S.ᵗ George   I.ᵉ Upright
M. Dromadaire
aux Anses
I.ᵉ des Rois   I. N. ou Kole ou de Surville
C. du N.O.   de Tasman   ou C. Maria   Sandy
de Van-Diemen   Port Marion, ou B. des Isles, ou de Lauriston
Bret ou Quarré
I. Barrière
C. Colvil
C. du Mercure
Cour des Aldermans
C. de l'Abondance
... de la Fui
fausse Baye   ... Est
B. de Tolaga
C. Howe   P.ᵗ Albatros
Ram-Head   B. de la Pauvreté
P.ᵗ Hicks   C. Runaway
Terre de   I.ᵉ Fourneaux
NOUVELLE   Détroit de Coo
I. Table ou Teraki   Kidnappers

I. de Noël

I. de Jesus

e d'Yorc

ARCHIPEL

I.' des Marquises de Mendoces

La Dominique
ou Ohchova
St.e Christinne
ou Ohilshoo

Hood ou Techooai

St.e Pierre ou Onateayo

La Madeleine ou Whattarre-toah

I. Penrhyn
de Marshall.

de BOURBON ou de TAITI

I. du Danger
ou de S. Bernard
déc.te par Mendana
le 20 Aoust 1595

I. Bauman ou Toutéepa

les Navigateurs
tué M. de Langle

I. Tiokea ou Oura
Anna   ou du Roy ou Georges
ou I.e du P.ce de Galles
ou I.e Per. supérieure
I. Waterland
ou Wahei
I.e Palliser ou Palai

I. sans fond

I. du Disappointement
ou Rima-roa

I. des Chiens
déc. par le Maire
le 10 Aout 1615

I.
Howe
I.
Morua
I. Scilly
I. Raictea
I. de Charl. Saunders
ou Tabbu-a-manua

I.
Tupia
I. Belabola
I. Otietea

I. Maurhyne
Op...tio
I. Taroa
de Venus

I. Carlehoff

I. de
l'Aventure
ou Taiti
I. Furneaux
ou Whaiva

ARCHIPEL DANGEREUX

I. Doutteuse
I. Revolution
de la Harpe

Les Lanciere

I. Palmerston
ou Rimalema

I. Whatootuakée
déc.te par Bligh en 1789
I. Hervei ou Mocno-tayo

I. de Dy Chean
I. Mistea ou en Hoova-nooe
I. Birds les 4 Grouppes
de l'Oiseau
ou Whao   ou du
P.ce Henry

I. de l'Arc

Les 4 Facardins

Les 4 Facardins
La Reine Charlotte

I. Lagon
I. Gloceter   La Pentecote
I. Egmont

I. Sauvage
ou Hitte-Potto

I. Atokootaya

I. Taiti   Oznabrug

I. Cumberland

I. Wateoo

I. Toometoa-roana
ou de Glocester

Isles de la Société

I. Mangea ou
Te-Oroora Mativatea

I. Ohite-roa

I. Hitte-tanaroo-eiroo
ou Oznabrug

I. Toobovai
ou Moutou

I. de l'Incarnation
vue par Quiros
le 18 Janvier 1605

I. Pitcairn

I.

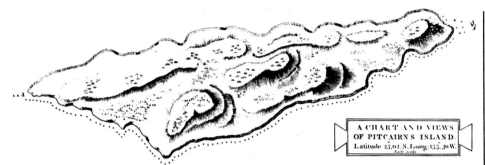

A CHART AND VIEWS
OF PITCAIRN'S ISLAND.
Latitude 25.02.S. Long: 133.30 W.

Previous spread: Map used during the voyage of Monsieur de Surville, Captain of the 'Vaisseaux'
Above: Carteret's chart of Pitcairn Island showing incorrect latitude

Undaunted, Christian determined to establish a colony there. For this to be successful, willing women were needed. He therefore sailed the *Bounty* 480 miles north to Tahiti, where he, Alexander Smith and probably Quintal were reunited with their actual or de facto wives.

Again enraptured with the sensual delights of Tahiti, some of the mutineers were tempted to stay there, but Christian was convinced that Bligh's revenge would trace them to Tahiti, and managed to convince the entire crew to stick to his plan to return to Toobouai.

How wives were obtained for the unmarried men may never be proven, but it seems highly likely that most of them were lured aboard on the night of 28th of September and kidnapped, along with six Tahitian men. This strange agglomeration of humanity, accompanied by 312 hogs, 38 goats, eight dozen fowls, a bull and a cow, set forth for Toobouai, arriving nine days after Bligh had reached Coupang.

The *Bounty* met a warmer reception than had earlier greeted it. Some of the natives proudly wore around their necks spent bullets from the previous visit. They were from a different tribe and made enthusiastic protestations of friendship. Christian went through the motions of amity but immediately set out to build a fortress, purchasing the land with some red feathers brought from Tahiti. Fifty yards square, and surrounded by a formidable moat, the fort was defended by four-pounders and swivel guns from the *Bounty*. Over it proudly, albeit ironically, flew the Union Jack.

The mutineers' first mistake was to unleash hundreds of pigs, which not only terrified the natives but rooted mercilessly through their crops. Even more fateful was something of which they were scarcely aware: their white skin and imperious behaviour so impressed the natives that it was bound to alienate their priests. This threatened oligarchy initiated a rumour which spread like fever: the moat, as yet unfilled, was designed by the Europeans to be a mass grave in which the entire native population was to be buried!

An attack by 700 natives was repulsed†, but Christian's control over his crew was gradually being eroded. The men demanded more leisure, more women, more grog. They broke into the Spirit Room and, thus fortified, spent three days in debate which resulted in a majority voting to return to Tahiti.

Christian agreed and left Toobouai, never to return. In September 1789, he landed 16 of the mutineers back in Tahiti, well armed and provisioned. Nine elected to stay with the *Bounty*. Initially, 26 others sailed with him – six Polynesian men, 19 women and one baby. One woman leaped overboard and swam to shore. Six others were put ashore at Moorea, all, according to Isaac Martin's wife‡, Jenny, 'rather ancient'!

The 28 remaining set sail in search of haven.

Somewhere in the 70,000,000 square

miles of scantily explored Pacific ocean, there had to be a place to hide. Christian criss-crossed the Pacific three times, visiting the Society, Austral, Tonga, Fiji and Cook groups, eventually sailing 7800 miles. On the way, he discovered Raratonga, where he introduced the orange tree whose juice is today its most important export.

The *Bounty*'s visit to the Cook Islands was remembered by the natives for generations.††

They spoke in awe of the appearance of a 'floating island' upon which grew 'two large plantations' (proof that not all the breadfruit was ditched by the mutineers) and which contained 'two rivers of water'. (The pumps, we assume, were in use at the time.)

In the first days of 1790, Christian arrived at the spot where one of Bligh's charts told him Pitcairn's Isle should be, to find nothing but further boundless stretches of water.

Yet this was to be their salvation. As Pitcairn had been incorrectly charted by Carteret, it was as good as undiscovered. If he could now find it, he would find precious oblivion. Zig-zagging for two hundred nautical miles west along the line of latitude, he came at last, on the 15th of January, in sight of Pitcairn's Isle.

Formidable as Norfolk Island's cliffs had appeared to La Perouse and King, these were far more so. For an agonising 48 hours, they feared that landing might be impossible but finally, on the western coast, they sighted a possible foothold. Christian, Brown, Williams, McCoy and three Polynesian men rowed ashore and surfed the skiff through wild waves to finally plant their sea-weary legs on land.

Their two days' exploration of the island produced incredibly good news. Four wooden images and some stone axes gave evidence of a much earlier habitation but there were now no people, no animals and, perhaps the greatest blessing of all, no mosquitos.

Utter loneliness was here but also peace and a wild beauty. The island was a great plateau, pierced by ravines two hundred feet in depth and crowned with ridges five hundred feet high and a peak which soared to a thousand.

The lush tangle of tropical vegetation was laced with ferns and vines and fragrant-blossoming shrubs, including the *tefano*, beloved of the Tahitian women. Thrusting their noble crowns above this undergrowth were giant causarinas and banyans, life-supporting coconut palms and breadfruit and pandanus trees. Fruit and vegetables grew wild. There was water. There were fish, shellfish and crayfish. With all this and the pigs, goats and chickens from the *Bounty*, they could live like pagan gods. Paradise had been regained.

The 28 refugees spent two weeks stripping the *Bounty* of everything moveable: sails for temporary tent-houses, oak for permanent dwellings, the ship's kettle for stews and, fatefully, for the brewing of grog. Goats, pigs,

---

† *Alexander Smith, alias John Adams, was captured by the Toobouaians but rescued. Had he not been, it is interesting to speculate on who would have been the last survivor on Pitcairn and whether, under the leadership of a Quintal or McCoy, they would have grown into 'the world's most perfect and pious race'!*

In another footnote to history, the brig 'Mercury' passed within two miles of Toobouai without detecting the presence of the mutineers.

‡ *Formerly Alexander Smith's*

†† *Recorded by John Williams in his 'Narrative of Missionary Enterprise in the South Sea Islands'.*

fowls, cats and dogs were swum ashore. (The latter were later destroyed for fear that their barking would reveal signs of occupancy to a passing vessel.) The baby, Sully, now a little over a year old, was said to have been transported ashore in a barrel.

From the Landing Place, the salvaged goods were backpacked and hauled up the formidable slope known to this day as the Hill of Difficulty, and a settlement was established on The Edge, a ledge of level ground overlooked by the Polynesian gods in their ancient *marae*.

All were agreed that the *Bounty* had to be got rid of 'to remove her giveaway silhouette

from the sight of retribution for Eternity'. Christian was for running her ashore for further stripping; others were more anxious. On the 23rd January, 1790, one of the crew, probably Quintal, took the matter into his own hands and set her afire.

Now the die was truly cast.

Just 55 days later, the *Sirius*, flagship of the First Fleet, which had sailed from England in the same year as the *Bounty*, was also to come to a melancholy end. As she approached death on a Norfolk Island reef, Bligh was arriving back in England to seek the death of the men who had so sorely bruised his ego.

Below: View of Pitcairn from Smyth's wonderful diary, made during the voyage of the 'Blossom'

CHAPTER 7

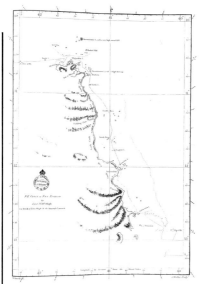

Pursuit

Valuable insights into Bligh's character are the venomous letters he proceeded to write to the relatives of the mutineers.

To an uncle of Midshipman Peter Heywood, who was a stripling of 16 years at the time of the mutiny, and took no active part in it, he wrote:

...your nephew, Peter Heywood, is amongst the mutineers. His ingratitude to me is of the blackest dye, for I was a father to him in every respect ... as his conduct always gave me much pleasure ...

I very much regret that so much Baseness formed the character of a young man I had real regard for, and it will give me much pleasure to hear his friends can bear the loss of him without much concern.

To Heywood's distraught mother, he offered these 'condolences':

Madam, I received your letter this day and feel for you very much, being perfectly sensible

of the extreme distress you must suffer from the conduct of your son, Peter. His baseness is beyond all description, but I hope you will endeavour to prevent the loss of him, heavy as the misfortune is, from afflicting you too severely.

Desire for revenge became so consuming that Bligh was apparently able to convince himself that all those who had stayed on board the *Bounty* were equally guilty. This was the impression given to those about to set out in pursuit of the mutineers, with appalling consequences.

In his original manuscript appears this statement: 'As for the officers, they endeavoured to come to my assistance, but were not allowed to put their heads above the hatchway.' It was omitted from his official narrative, one can only assume by deliberate intent.

George III swiftly despatched H.M.S.

Far left: Captain Edward Edwards – from a camera portrait
Left: Bligh's sketch map of the Great Barrier Reef which he successfully negotiated but which Edwards did not
Below: Admission by Bligh in his original MS – later deleted

to have retaken her, and that as to the Pistols he was so fluried and surprized that he did not recollect he had them. — His Brother said on my enquiring how the Keys of the Arm Chest came out of his Cabbin, that Richard Skinner who attended on him had taken them away which was certainly the case.

As for the Officers whose Cabbins were in the Cockpitt, there was no relief for them — they endeavoured to come to my Assistance; but were not allowed to put their heads above the Hatchway. —

The Boatswain and Carpenter were fully at liberty — the former was employed on pain of death to hoist the Boats out, but the latter

Pandora to capture the mutineers. She was under the command of Captain Edward Edwards, a man compared with whom Bligh was a saint. He sailed to the obvious place — Tahiti — and had no trouble capturing those of the *Bounty*'s crew who had returned there.

Their sojourn had not proved to be as paradisiacal as they had imagined. Heywood and Stewart, convinced of their ability to prove their non-involvement in the mutiny, were content to enjoy a quiet life whilst awaiting the inevitable arrival of a British man-o'-war. Heywood filled much of his time in compiling an English/Polynesian dictionary. Stewart had formally married a chief's daughter and settled down to marital bliss which was soon rewarded with a daughter.

Some of the others became mercenaries in the service of the Tahitian boy-king, Tu, and, between skirmishes, laboured mightily to build an escape-boat.

Another group, led by Charles Churchill and his vicious lieutenant Matt Thompson, spent their days in disposing of the rum rations left them by Christian, then indulged in pillage and rape to the point where they were obliged to flee to another part of the island. Here they somehow convinced the natives that their chief, who had mysteriously disappeared, had appointed Churchill his successor.

Churchill fell out with Thompson over the disappearance of his musket and Thompson murdered him. In some strange logic of retribution, the natives turned on Thompson. Beguiling him with pleas to become their new king, they got between him and his musket, pinned him to the sand with a branch, beat him to death with stones and beheaded him.

The boat-building continued and by the 30th of April the 30-foot vessel was fully planked and caulked with breadfruit gum. She was launched with due ceremony, named *Resolution*, and blessed by the native priests who believed she was to become the key to their dominance over their rivals. The Englishmen, to demonstrate their loyalty and remove any suspicion of their desire to escape, sailed the *Resolution* (in company with forty war-canoes) into battle against the forces of a rival chief. They won.

Tu now demanded the surrender of all the kingdoms on the island. Most capitulated and their chiefs exhibited their fealty at a ceremony in which thirty human sacrifices were offered. The boy-king sat throughout this picnic with his mouth lolling open in symbol of cannibalistic power.

The ensuing festivities and monumental banquet were interrupted by the arrival of the *Pandora*.

Edwards had no difficulty in rounding up all of the mutineers — Midshipmen Heywood and Stewart, Boatswain's Mate Morrison, Carpenter's Mate Norman, Carpenter's Crew M'Intosh, Armourer Coleman and Seamen Skinner, Ellison, Hillibrant, Burkett, Millward, Sumner, Muspratt and Byrne. Having accepted Bligh's portrayal of the entire crew as villains, he showed mercy to none. On the ship's quarterdeck he ordered the building of the infamous *Pandora's Box* — a construction 18 feet by 11 feet, only just taller than a man and entered by a scuttle in the roof, about 18 inches square.

In this airless and fetid prison, 14 men were incarcerated for sixty days.

Boatswain's Mate James Morrison, in a memorandum headed *Vidi et Scio* (I saw and I know), wrote:

. . . the heat was so intense that the Sweat . . . ran in Streams down the Scuppers, and soon produced Maggots . . . This and two necessary Tubs which were kept in the Box, made it truly disagreeable.

Edwards spent three months searching for the *Bounty,* and actually sighted Dulcie Island, 500 kilometres to the west of Pitcairn, which, on the scale of the Pacific, was close. He finally decided to abandon the hunt and headed for Timor via the Great Barrier Reef. Here, he ran *Pandora* aground. With the ship breaking up around them, he refused to release the prisoners from the Box, ordering the guards to fire on them at the least sign of motion. When one of the crew finally ripped off the hatch, it was too late for all to escape and four of the manacled prisoners perished.†

The survivors sheltered from the fierce sun in tents made from sails, all but the ten prisoners whom Edwards banned from shelter, even refusing them the use of an old sail. With the sun searing skin bleached white by months of confinement in the Box, they buried themselves to the neck in sand but, as Peter Heywood later wrote, they all 'soon apeared as if dipped in . . . tubs of boiling water'.

There followed a journey, one-third of the distance covered by Bligh, and by no means so well organised, in which 99 men in four open boats sailed to the haven of Coupang. The prisoners, irrespective of guilt, all spent an incredible 15 months in irons.

Ten of them were finally taken to trial. Seven were exonerated or pardoned and three, Ellison, Millward and Burkett (the seaman reputed to have endeavoured to save Bligh from humiliation by covering his nakedness), were hanged from the yard-arm of a prison hulk on the Thames. Thousands hired boats for family outings on the river to witness the hangings.

But no one was to set eyes on the Pitcairners for 18 years.

† *The 21-gun frigate has recently been discovered lying in 17 fathoms (33 metres) of water on the outer edge of the reef near the tip of Cape York. A veil of coarse sand has preserved her so well that the Federal and Queensland governments have launched a rescue project which may result in her being raised intact to become a feature of Australia's bicentenary in 1988.*

Above: Etching of the wreck of the 'Pandora' – made after a sketch by Midshipman Peter Heywood

CHAPTER 8

Commandants and Convicts

By the year 1790, the population of Norfolk Island had swollen to 150 and it was soon to quadruple. On the way were another 183 convicts, 27 of their children, two companies of marines and a new Commandant, Lt. Governor Major Robert Ross. They were being transported in the *Sirius*, the flagship of the First Fleet, and the smaller *Supply*.

At Cascade Bay, so named by Captain Cook for its waterfall, the ships managed to discharge most of their human complement but *Sirius* was prevented by foul weather from unloading her considerable stores and provisions. Captain Hunter then sailed to the other side of the island and hove to offshore, hoping to return and discharge her cargo in more favourable conditions.

Sirius met her fate off Point Ross, on the reef which Commandant King had pleaded to have removed. Following a sudden shift in the wind, the flagship was impaled on the teeth of the coral and, from that moment, was doomed.

A rope was tied to a keg and surfed to the shore where it was used to haul ashore a stout hawser which was fixed to a tree below the property known today as *Ross-haven*. A 'traveller' was attached to the hawser and two convicts were instructed to haul themselves out to the wreck and salvage the stores. In the hold of the foundering *Sirius*, they discovered something worth dying for – grog! As they caroused the day away, another convict volunteer was despatched via the hawser to save the situation but much of the cargo was lost, leaving the beleaguered island with 500 additional mouths to feed.† What happened to the two carousers is strangely not recorded.

The ban on vessels of sufficient seaworthiness to cope with Norfolk's waters meant that fishing could normally only be carried out from the shore. Food became so scarce that convicts were known to consume an entire week's rations in one meal. As the spectre of

† *Two of the ship's cannons today flank the steps of the Administration offices in the New Military Barracks. Her largest anchor was located in 1985 by a diving team from Australia and is destined for Norfolk's new museum.*

Far left: Watercolour by Lieutenant William Bradley of the 'Sirius', showing the cable linked to the shore
Left: H.M.S. 'Sirius'. 'Safely moored in Sydney Cove' – G. C. Ingleton
Below: Anchor from 'Sirius'
Bottom: View of Sydney (Kingston) in 1796 – W. N. Chapman

Above: 'Norfolk Island Petrel'

kept records showed a total of 171,362 birds slain. Finally, the remaining few thousand reputedly shifted their breeding grounds to Lord Howe, never to return to Norfolk.†

But while life was assured, punishment, of course, continued.

The cat-o'-nine-tails usually broke the flesh on the fourth blow. If a man fainted on the triangle before he had received his prescribed number of lashes, he was taken down and the remainder saved for a time when he was able to bear them. If the flogger did not wield the lash with appropriate zeal, he himself would be flogged. At no time did it appear to occur to the Commandants of this moralistic establishment that men suffering from bestial conditions and deplorable hunger cannot work indefinitely. To eat, they stole. To retain some vestige of self-respect, they were insubordinate. This led to more punishment, condoned, to a large degree, by the chaplains who conducted Divine Service every Sunday to an audience who must have wondered whether God was dead.

A letter from a Commandant's wife‡ offers insight into the attitude of the upper classes to their subordinates. These are not not the thoughts of a uniquely insensitive person but rather of a woman who would consider herself as humane as any other of her class:

The Major's turn came for doing duty at Norfolk Island as Commandant, and we went to that terrestrial paradise, where the clanking of chains and the fall of the lash rang in the ear from daylight till dark – these sounds accompanied occasionally by the report of a discharged musket, and the shriek of some wretch who had fallen mortally wounded.

These shots became so frequent that at last they ceased to disturb us, even at our meals.

starvation hovered over Norfolk, salvation arrived overnight. Like manna to the Israelites, hundreds of thousands of shearwaters appeared from the sky, migrating back to their nesting burrows on Mount Pitt.

The starving islanders called them 'Birds of Providence', believing they were sent by God to save them. For months, these fishy-tasting but life-preserving birds were slaughtered in numbers between two and three thousand each night. Despite this wholesale decimation, the birds remained so curious that they would come to the feet of club-bearing men at a call. Between April and July of 1795, the carefully

Our house was behind rampart, surmounted by a battery of guns, loaded to the muzzles with bullets, bits of iron, tenpenny nails, and tenter-hooks. By day and night sentries guarded the door with loaded muskets and fixed bayonets.

'Kill the Commandant' was always the first article of the agreement these desperate monsters came to when they entertained an idea of escape.

In the morning when they were brought out heavily ironed to go to work, the guard that had been on duty came from the barracks, and, in the presence of the Commandant, obeyed the order, 'Prime and load'. Then came the ringing of the iron ramrod in the barrel. Then the order, 'Fix bayonets', followed by the flashing of the bright steel in the sun's rays.

Many a time have I, from my window, seen these incorrigibles smile and grin during this ceremony, albeit they knew that upon very slight provocation they would receive the bullet or taste the steel. During the twelve months that we were on the island, one hundred and nine were shot by the sentries in self-defence and sixty-three bayoneted to death, while the average number of lashes administered every day was six hundred.

Yet, to my certain knowledge, almost every officer who acted as Commandant at Norfolk Island tried to be as lenient as possible, but soon discovered that, instead of making matters better, they make them worse, and they were, in consequence, compelled to resort, for security's sake, to the ready use of the bullet and the bayonet, and the constant use of the lash.

† Or so it was thought. 185 years after the last Bird of Providence was sighted in the environs of Norfolk, a small breeding colony has returned. It was discovered on 15th July, 1985, by the Government Conservator, Neil Hermes, on Philip Island, four miles offshore. (Over the years, the original name of Phillip Island lost one of its 'l's.)

‡ 'Recollections by a Commandant's Wife' from 'Fragments of the Early History of Australia, from 1788 to 1812' – Mitchell Library

Below: 'The Convict System' – 'Australasian Sketchbook'

That part of the punishment which galled these wretched prisoners most was the perpetual silence that was insisted upon. They were not allowed to speak a word to each other.

One day, when the Major was inspecting them, they addressed him through a spokesman, who had been originally a surgeon, and who had been transported for a most diabolical offence. He was a very plausible man, and made a most ingenious speech, which finished thus:

'Double, if you will, the weight of our irons and our arm-chains, reduce the amount of the food we now receive by way of ration, but, in the name of humanity, permit us the use of our tongues and our ears, that we may at least have the consolation of confessing to each other the justice of the punishment we have to undergo.'

The Major turned a deaf ear to this harangue and, when he related it to me, laughed at it. I, however, foolishly took a different view of the case, and teased him into trying the effect of such indulgence. What was the result? The use they made of their tongues was to concoct a plan for butchering the *garrison and every free man and seizing the next vessel that brought a fresh cargo of convicts to the island.*

In 1791, Commandant King returned for a second term. High on his list of priorities was the problem of how to make use of the flax which Captain Cook had hoped would be woven into sails for His Majesty's Navy. To this end, the British Government initiated an escapade which turned into a farce.

In the first recorded instance of black-birding in the South Pacific, the captain of H.M.S. *Daedalus* was despatched to New Zealand with orders reading: '. . . you are to use your best endeavours to take with you one or two of the natives of that country versed in the operations necessary for the manufacture of the flax-plant of which their garments are mostly made . . .'

Two Maoris, Woodoo and Tookee, were duly enticed on board, invited below decks to inspect some trade goods and kidnapped. One turned out to be a priest, the other a warrior. They knew almost nothing about flax-making, considering it 'women's work'. King had the grace to return the two unfortunates to their homeland and abandoned the hope of realising Cook's dream. Cook's other idea — of using Norfolk Pine for masts — also proved to be impractical, though the timber made stout hulls.

Norfolk's population was now over a thousand and to command it for the next four years came the relatively benign Captain Townson. The Captain's bravest act was to ignore the ban on building boats and to construct a 25-ton sloop he defiantly named *Norfolk*. He despatched her to Sydney with pleas to Governor Hunter that food and clothing

should be sent to Norfolk urgently. Hunter earmarked another vessel for that purpose and promptly commandeered the *Norfolk*, passing her over to the redoubtable Matthew Flinders and George Bass who used her to circumnavigate Van Diemen's Land, proving it an island separate from Australia.

They reported that the convict craftsmen who had built the little Norfolk pine sloop had done well. 'Seas that were apparently determined to swallow her,' wrote Flinders, 'she rode over with all the ease and majesty of an old and experienced petterel'.

Eventually, while on a cargo run on the Hawkesbury river, she was seized by a party of convicts whose plan was to sail the tiny vessel to China. Instead, they managed to run her ashore at the mouth of the Hawkesbury where she broke up.

† *For this blessing, the locals are duly thankful — otherwise Norfolk might have become as bare as its neighbour, Phillip Island.*

Far left: Leg irons
Left: Maori flax-making. From an 1846 painting by G. F. Angas
Below: Matthew Flinders

When tales of benign rulership filtered back to Britain, the authorities tut-tutted with disbelief and, in 1800, appointed a new Commandant, the tyrant Major Foveaux.

Having made a vast fortune as the head of the New South Wales Police Corps by dint of exploiting the convicts on his properties, Foveaux instituted a system of encouraging stool-pigeons. Thus it was that a rapist called Gready was encouraged to inform on a party of convicts who, he claimed, had aggregated a cache of 100 pikes and were about to use them. On the word of this dubious witness, Foveaux made an instant example of two Irish dissidents

Below right: The flogging of Charles Maher – watercolour and description from the notebook of Robert Jones

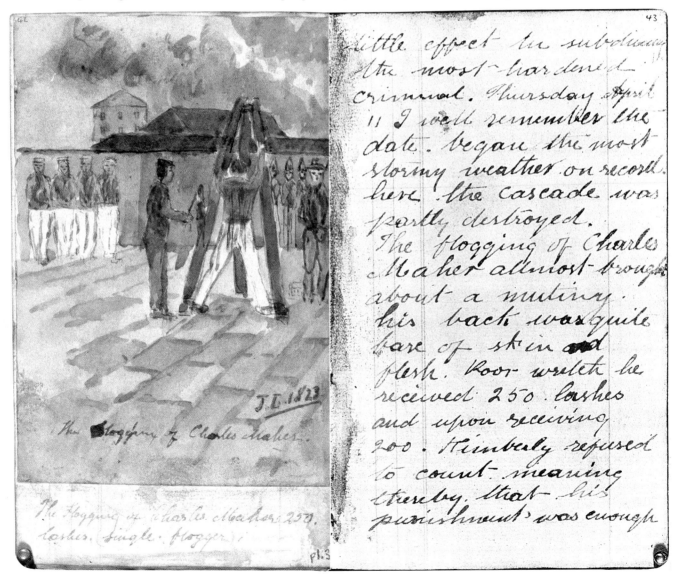

The Flogging of Charles Maher.

J.D. 1823

The Flogging of Charles Maher. 250. lashes. Single. flogger.

little effect on subduing the most hardened criminal. Thursday April 11 I well remember the date. began the most stormy weather on record here. the cascade was partly destroyed.

The flogging of Charles Maher almost brought about a mutiny. his back was quite bare of skin and flesh. Poor wretch he received 250. lashes and upon receiving 200. Kimberly refused to count. meaning thereby. that his punishment was enough he suspected of being ringleaders and hung them, without trial, that very night.

And then began an orgy of flogging. One unfortunate, named Joe Malmsbury, received 2000 lashes in a period of three years. His back was quite bare of flesh and his exposed collarbones looked 'very much like two ivory polished horns'. It was with some difficulty that Foveaux could find another place to flog him and he is reported to have said, 'Next time we'd better try the soles of his feet'. The Chief Constable, Ted Kimberley, was reported to say, as he laid on the lash, 'Another half-pound off the beggar's ribs!'

Major Foveaux is reported to have had a passion for witnessing punishments. An emancipated convict testified that he would 'often order some poor wretch to the triangle and laugh at his cries for mercy'. Women were not merely flogged, they were stripped naked and surrounded by male convicts, encouraged in their hoots and yells by the gloating Commandant.

All of this activity was maliciously abetted by Foveaux's mistress, whom Foveaux took to live with him under threat to her husband that he would suffer horribly if a word of complaint was heard from him. 'Sauciness' to Foveaux's lady was instantly rewarded on the triangle. Twenty-five lashes was her usual retribution but one day she sentenced a particularly envious convict woman to 250.

Even the case-hardened Chief Constable Kimberley could not handle this particular hypocrisy. He hurled down the cat and yelled, 'I don't flog women!'

Foveaux ordered a soldier to deliver the 250 blows and then, noting that her back was insufficiently scarred for his delectation, ordered that she should be cast into solitary confinement. At this point the Assistant Surgeon stepped forward and suggested that sufficient punishment had been delivered. No priest is reported to have lifted a hand.

Now, to Norfolk, came the dashing Captain John Piper. The vulture, Foveaux, had been replaced by a peacock, but Piper was to oversee

Below: John Piper

the period which was probably the island's happiest, from 1804 to 1810.

Captain Piper's task was a relatively easy one. His instructions were to wind up – or wind down – the colony. And, fortunately for the convicts, Piper's predilections tended towards the pursuit of pleasure rather than pain. He found the girls on the island as eager, perhaps, as those that the *Bounty*'s crew had found on Tahiti. In a note to a friend he averred: 'I need help; the girls are too much for me'. The one who most engaged his affections was a lively 15-year-old named Mary Ann Shears, the daughter of a couple of First Fleet convicts, with whom he proceeded to found a mini-dynasty of ten children.

Below: The watermill in Arthur's Vale, 1796 – W. N. Chapman

Piper was the first inhabitant of Norfolk's imposing Government House, built by Foveaux, and he lived in grandiloquent style. His only real challenge came during 1804. This was the time of the Napoleonic Wars, and when the Commandant was informed that a fleet of nine ships was approaching Norfolk, he assumed them to be French warships and had one of his few cannons hauled across the island from Kingston to Cascade. But ammunition was the problem. Piper had the island scoured for bottles which were broken up and loaded into the gun. It transpired that the fleet was British, lately out of China.

Among the Captain's more colourful 'guests' were more than sixty Irish dissidents, the ringleader of whom was Sir Henry Brown Hayes, an Irish knight who was transported originally to Botany Bay, allegedly for abducting a Quaker heiress but probably for political reasons. Sir Henry was wealthy and well-connected and thus better treated than most. He asked permission to found the first Freemasons' Lodge in Australia, was refused, but went ahead. Sentenced to a term of hard labour in Van Diemen's Land, he filled in the time whilst waiting for a ship to transport him by buying 42 acres of land at Vaucluse, building a magnificent home and planting thousands of fruit trees on the property. He was eventually sent to Norfolk Island and the property, Vaucluse House, subsequently passed to William Charles Wentworth, explorer, statesman and poet, who had been born on Norfolk, the son of Surgeon D'Arcy Wentworth.

Piper is also remembered in the name of a ritzy Sydney neighbourhood – Point Piper. At the expiration of his Norfolk term, he became Collector of Customs in Sydney, receiving, in lieu of salary, 5% of all he collected. This cosy arrangement enabled him to build a mansion on the point whose *pièce de résistance* was a magnificent domed ballroom for which the dashing captain retained a permanent orchestra.

An enquiry into his wealth led to Piper's sacking whereupon he staged one of Sydney's more spectacular protests: in the middle of Sydney Harbour he hurled himself from his private barge into the waves, to the accompaniment of what is reputed to have been Handel's Water Music. As arranged, the musicians rescued him, but from then on his fortunes took a decided downturn.

In 1808, while Piper was awaiting his transfer from Norfolk, the *Lady Nelson* arrived at Norfolk to transfer some settlers to Van Diemen's Land. She had been despatched there by none other than Captain Bligh . . .

Below: 'View of Sydney on the South Side of Norfolk Island' – Edward Dayes. State Library of Victoria

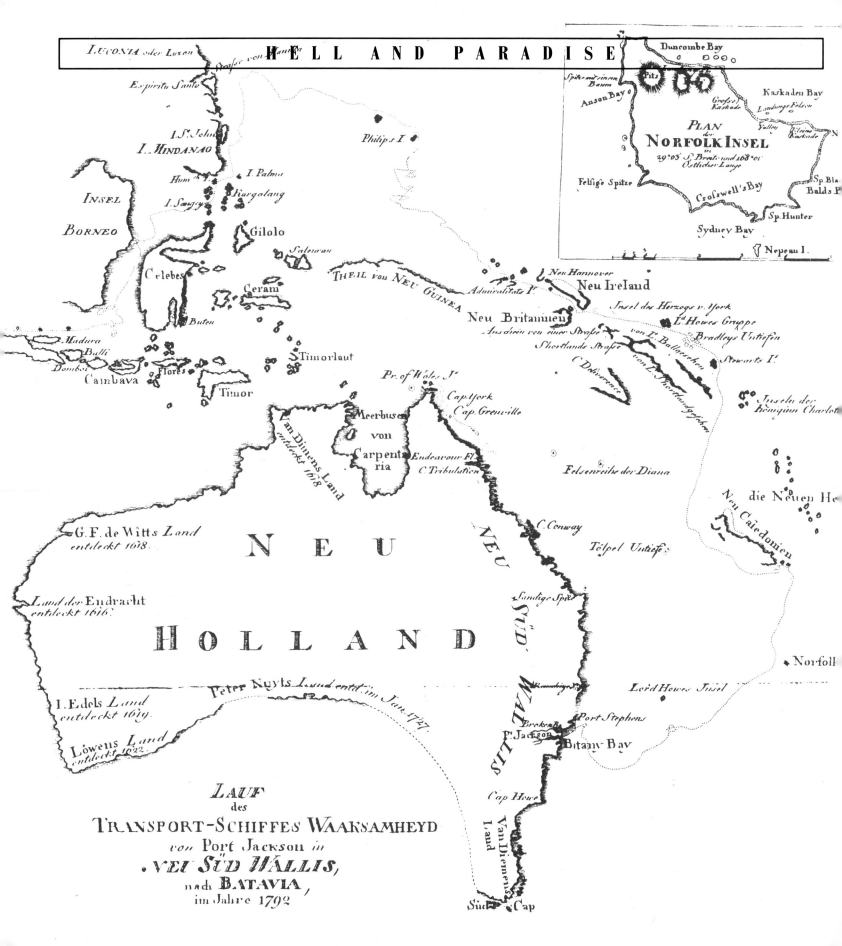

CHAPTER 9

William Bligh Again

Bligh's despatch to Norfolk of the *Lady Nelson* was a mistake triggered by the overconfidence that continually warped his judgment.

Since his return to England to a hero's welcome in 1790, his life had been an astonishing amalgam of triumph and humiliation.

He was invited to an audience with King George III and fêted at a series of banquets. Through the offices of Sir Joseph Banks, he was granted a gratuity of 500 guineas by the Jamaican House of Assembly in appreciation of his efforts to provide cheap food for the plantation slaves. His book *A Voyage to the South Sea, undertaken by the command of His Majesty, for the Purpose of Conveying the Breadfruit Tree to the West Indies*, was an instant bestseller. He was promoted to commander and, a few weeks later, to post-captain, and appointed to lead a second breadfruit expedition which was successful and rewarded him with a further gratuity of a thousand guineas.

But during his absence from Britain, the trial of the mutineers had been held and public opinion had turned against him. He had sown the seeds of his destruction during the triumphal period prior to his leaving when he chose to ignore the fact that Peter Heywood's family was rich, talented and well-connected. When, claiming that the 16-year-old Midshipman's 'baseness' was 'beyond all description', he had advised Heywood's uncle that 'it will give me great pleasure to hear that his friends can bear the loss of him without much concern', he had badly undervalued the calibre of his opposition.

The Heywoods joined with the equally influential Christians – in particular, Fletcher's highly articulate lawyer brother, Edward – making sure that the right people were lobbied and that those under trial were strongly represented. The mutineers, to a man, testified that young Heywood was innocent. Not only was

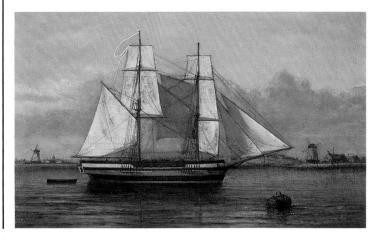

Far left: 1792 map of New Holland with insert suggesting the interest of 'other foreign powers' in the island. National Maritime Museum, England
Above left: Captain Bligh – George Dance, 1794. National Maritime Museum, England
Below : H.M.S. 'Lady Nelson'

he acquitted but he was promoted, eventually contributing 42 years of distinguished service to the Navy and rising to the rank of Admiral. The dictionary of the Polynesian language which he compiled in Tahiti was published and lent further support to the idea that a good man would have ended his life on a yard-arm had Bligh had his way. Bligh's eccentric behaviour, in particular the incident of the 'stolen' coconuts, was well ventilated and witness after witness attested to his proclivity to humiliate his subordinates.

Following the trial, Edward Christian pressed home a remorseless campaign to damage Bligh's integrity. He published a brilliantly argued *Appendix* to the Minutes of the Proceedings which pointed out that even those who, at his brother Fletcher's instigation, had suffered so terribly in the open boat journey spoke of him not only 'without resentment and with forgiveness' but 'with a degree of rapture and enthusiasm'. 'There is a degree of pressure', he concluded, 'beyond which the best formed and principled mind must either break or recoil'.†

As a result of all this publicity, Bligh's hero status was swiftly transmogrified into that of a baleful tyrant. No half-measures and no half-opinions ever mellowed his life. But half rations were to be his lot for almost two years whilst he was unemployed by the Navy, fretting in port while his fellow captains were garnering glory in battles against France and Holland.

When he was at length allowed to return to the sea, it was not long before he was involved in another mutiny (his third, if we can consider the incident in the Whitsundays a mutiny‡).

But this time he was not alone; the entire Nore Fleet mutinied and demands for their removal were faced by all unpopular officers. Nevertheless, Bligh was tipped off a ship under his command for the second time. This time he escaped, justifiably, without public censure.

By the time of the battle of Camperdown, his obvious abilities had outweighed his unpopularity with the Admiralty and he was given a chance to refurbish his reputation. He displayed splendid bravery and superb seamanship in taking his ship, *Director*, on a solo dash through the thick of the fighting to engage the Dutch flagship. As luck would have it, Admiral Duncan's division was already well in command of the situation but Bligh, not realising this, proceeded to finish off the stricken vessel. For this action he was accused of 'presumptuous poaching'. The fact that he had brought *Director* through with only seven casualties and not a single death was interpreted to mean that he had shirked the real action in order to get in at the kill and reap the glory.

Unaware of or insensitive to this reaction, Bligh was, for a time, a proud and happy man, until he was struck with rheumatism, possibly a legacy of his open boat journey. This affliction, characterised by 'an alarming numbness of the left arm', plagued him but, in relieving him of some of his seaboard duties, gave him the time to perfect his invention, a new kind of compass. For all Bligh's illustrious reputation as a navigator, it was ignored by the Admiralty.

This did nothing to appease his irascibility and during his final days with *Director* he was involved in a clash with its Master, John Ramsay, which culminated in another court-martial. The result was an implied criticism by the court: Bligh received another Master, Ramsay another ship.

But now came another opportunity for Bligh to prove himself in battle and, this time, it was an unalloyed triumph. At the battle of Copenhagen, Nelson gave Bligh the most honoured battle station – plumb opposite the Danish flagship *Dannebroge*, where he performed with magnificent initiative, courage and loyalty to Nelson.

At Commander-in-Chief Parker's signal to retreat, Bligh took his cue from Nelson's famous 'blind-eye' reply and hurled his ship into point-blank combat with *Dannebroge*. They were engaged in a mutual bloody broadside for over two hours, Bligh suffering dreadful casualties but getting the better of it by dint of extremely skilful manoeuvring. When victory was won, Nelson hailed him aboard *Elephant* and publicly thanked him.

From this stirring achievement he emerged with a bad case of battle fatigue. Again he missed promotion. It was abysmal luck. During the scare of a Napoleonic invasion which preceded Trafalgar, he wished in vain for a command with the Channel Fleet. By the time he took command of *Warrior*, he was a searingly frustrated man. He took a dislike to yet another of his Masters, John Frazier, abusing him constantly in front of crew and officers. When Frazier had a fall and badly injured his leg, Bligh accused him of 'malingering'. 'What can I do?', Frazier was reported to reply, 'My God, I wish I was able to keep my watch!' Bligh promptly charged him with 'contumacy and disobedience' and placed him under arrest.

At the trial, Frazier testified that Bligh 'publicly on the quarter-deck ... did grossly insult and ill-treat me ... calling me rascal, scoundrel and shaking his fist in my face'. Bligh, in an act of self-conviction, asserted that all of

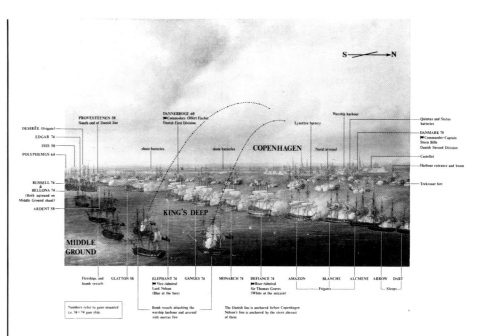

Above: Battle of Copenhagen – National Maritime Museum, England

his officers were 'worse than serpents'. He escaped with an admonishment but it was another rebuke, one that Bligh found harder to cope with than any mutiny. He wrote a forlorn letter to his ever-faithful patron, Sir Joseph Banks. Not even that illustrious figure could restore Bligh's naval career, but he came up with a remarkable offer, a post which appeared to offer Bligh the chance to restore his fortune and his self-esteem, if he had ever lost it. It was the Governorship of New South Wales.

† *Fletcher's brother Charles, in his autobiography, describes a conversation between a Manx friend and Bligh. When asked what could have led to Fletcher's defection, Bligh replied: 'It was Insanity'. 'He spoke right', says Charles, 'but who was it that drove him into that unhappy state?'*
‡ *See Chapter 5.*

Success to Major George Johnston;

May he live for ever! Our
Deliverer and Suppressor of
TYRANTS!

Above: Broadside issued by the
New South Wales mutineers. If
Bligh did indeed hide under a bed,
it was the only time in his career
that he failed in courage.

The whole idea of establishing a penal colony in New Holland had been Banks's. Amazingly, for such a gifted man, he believed that the convicts could 'maintain themselves, after the first year, with little or no aid from the mother country'. Indeed, they would become a market for England, they would 'naturally increase, and find occasion for many European commodities'. Instead, they almost starved to death.

After eight years, the colony had become relatively self-supporting but it was riddled with graft. The Governor, Captain Philip Gidley King, was by now a shell of the dashing young commandant who had founded the settlement on Norfolk Island.

Now elderly and gout-ridden, he was worn out by his battles with the military clique in endeavouring to break their sinecure on the sale of rum. He had also met a formidable adversary in John McArthur, the visionary but fiercely ambitious land-grabber who had beaten him with the trump card of Merino sheep.

Another person worn out by constant battle – in her case in constant defence of her husband – was Bligh's faithful and beloved wife, Betsy. It must have been anguishing for Bligh to leave her behind and face life alone for four years, but he needed an income and a challenge which would demonstrate to the world his true calibre.

Battle, of course, had never daunted Bligh, and within a week of sailing he was at it again. He was in charge of his own vessel, the *Lady Sinclair*, but subordinate to Captain Joseph Short, commander of the convoy. This subordination he refused to acknowledge. He was engaged in constant disputes about which route should be sailed, which stops should be

made and for how long. Short's early astonishment grew to outrage as Bligh's arrogance continued. He finally put his authority to the test in a hair-raising incident in which he directed the gunner to fire shots across *Lady Sinclair*'s bows when Bligh took it on a course different from the one Short had ordered. The third shot was to be fired directly at Bligh's ship should he refuse to divert. The gunner was Bligh's son-in-law.

Bligh lay low following this incident and planned his revenge. As soon as the fleet anchored in Sydney Cove, he became the supreme authority. In an act of pure spite, he informed Short that he was instantly relieving him of his command. When Short refused to leave ship, Bligh arrested him. He packed Short, his wife and family back to England, knowing that their entire possessions were in Sydney and being fully aware that the returning boat was a leaky, decrepit hulk. The rigours of the journey killed Short's wife and one of his children. It was cold comfort that he was honourably acquitted and Bligh severely censured.

Bligh, in the meantime, had his hands full. He was doing battle with the 'Rum Corps' to whom he had issued a stream of audacious orders designed to break their monopoly. But he had no back-up. Napoleon's victories in Europe were mounting and not one soldier could be spared from the battle zones.

True to form, he felt himself an impregnable rock in the ferment surrounding him. Had self-righteousness not prevented him from realising the extent of the hatred he was attracting, he would not have sent to Norfolk the last ship he had at Port Jackson. This left him without a naval influence to balance the power of the military officers who were on the point of insurgency. As soon as the *Lady Nelson* sailed, they arrested him.

Thus was Bligh the focus of his final mutiny and his final court-martial.

The *Lady Nelson* transported a number of convicts to Van Diemen's Land and, over the next six years, the remainder were gradually to join them.

As a result of the benign reign of Piper and his successors during the closing days of the settlement, the convicts had begun to look upon the Norfolk Island commandants as the devils they knew and a transfer to Van Diemen's Land raised the spectre of a tyrant in the mould of Morisset or Foveaux. In an attempt to make themselves too ill to be taken away, many of them drank gallons of sea water and ate pounds of sand. Five men died as a result and the rest were transported.

In February 1814, the last of the Government men and Free Settlers departed. To make sure that no foreign power should inherit them, the buildings, constructed with such grinding labour, were burned or razed. A dozen dogs were left on the island with the express role of killing the remaining cattle and pigs. When starvation approached, it was expected, they would 'turn and kill'.

Thus, in 1814, was the island left in peace. Only the headstones in her cemetery bore witness to the atrocities perpetrated against her. For an all-too-short time, Norfolk Island was allowed to revert to Paradise . . .

In a despatch to Viscount Castlereagh explaining that the 'Rum Rebellion' had come about as a result of his efforts to put down the illicit 'Spirit Traffic', Bligh claimed that the captain of a certain Yankee sealer, the *Topaz*, had sold to officers of His Majesty's Armed Ship

Above: William Bligh

Porpoise 950 gallons of rum and gin but that only 300 gallons were credited in the ship's log, the remainder being sold by the officers 'for two and three pounds a gallon'.

Little could Bligh have guessed, as he wrote those words, that the *Topaz* had since crossed the Pacific and solved the twenty-year mystery of the fate of the *Bounty*!

CHAPTER 10

Purgatory in Eden

After the burning of the *Bounty,* Fletcher Christian was faced with a social dilemma probably unique in history: how to mould a workable society from 18 Polynesians and nine Europeans marooned, probably forever, and each group almost totally ignorant of the other's language and culture.

It probably did not occur to him, any more than it would have to any Englishman of the day, that dark-skinned people should play any role other than that of 'hewers of wood and drawers of water' and he duly divided his new kingdom into nine parts, one for each of the Europeans. If he gave thought to the effect that sexual starvation might have on the Polynesian men, there was little he could do about it; after a wife had been allocated to each of the whites, only three were left to cater for six Polynesian men. They too had their hierarchies and Tararo, the highest born, took a woman, Toofaiti, for his own. Two others shared Mareva whilst Tinafanaea lived in a conflict-ridden union with three 'husbands'.

As Christian and Young, at least, were kind to their servants and Quintal and McCoy had not yet reduced them to the level of slaves, this unequal society survived without open hostility for about two years, until John Williams's wife was killed in a fall from a cliff and he demanded that Toofaiti, Tararo's wife, be handed over to him. He was temporarily dissuaded from this course by the promise that the child Sully would be his on her arrival at the age of puberty, that age being considered to be 11 or 12. Williams suffered celibacy for a time but eventually abducted the original object of his desire, arousing bitter resentment in the husband and several of the other Tahitians. Not unreasonably, they resolved to murder him – and all the other Englishmen.

Hints to their intentions were given by the white men's native wives in their working songs: 'Why does black man sharpen axe? To kill white man!' The first attempt was thwarted and, by order of Christian, the two ringleaders were shot by the Tahitian, Menallee.

A couple of years of relative harmony passed and more children were born. But the Polynesians, goaded by the extreme mis-treatment meted out to them by Quintal and McCoy (including having salt rubbed into the wounds inflicted by flogging), went on another rampage. Quintal and McCoy eluded them, but they succeeded in shooting, axing and stoning to death four of the whites, Williams, Mills, Martin and Brown. And probably a fifth – Fletcher Christian.

The actual cause and place of Christian's death may never be discovered. There is quite a

Far left: Lookout Ridge and Christian's house
Left: Pitcairn Island statue – Smyth

remarkable agreement about the details of the deaths of all the others but an equally remarkable disagreement about Christian's fate. Had he been slain by natives, there would seem to be no reason to have hidden the fact; indeed, it would be natural to expect that the day on which a community's leader dies will be remembered and hallowed. Yet every Pitcairner interviewed years later told a different story.

From the welter of conflicting stories told by the surviving Pitcairners, one can only guess at the facts. One version claimed that, driven insane from remorse and loneliness, Christian had thrown himself off the cliff on to the rocks.

Others insisted that he had survived the attempted shooting and recovered from his wounds in a cave which is to this day known as Christian's Cave.

Yet another claimed that he built a boat and escaped in it. A strange legend arose in England linking him with Coleridge's famous poem 'The Rime of the Ancient Mariner'.

It is true that Coleridge was a friend of Christian's parents and had planned to write something called 'The Adventures of Fletcher Christian'. (A notebook in the Public Records Office attests to this.) It is also just possible that Coleridge had some inside information shared by that other friend of the Christians – William Wordsworth. The latter wrote in 1796 to a publication called *The Weekly Entertainer* the only signed letter he is known to have sent to a newspaper:

Sir. There having appeared in your Entertainer (vide the 255th page of the present volume) an extract from a work purporting to be the production of Fletcher Christian, who headed the mutiny on board the Bounty; I think it proper to inform you that I have the best authority for saying that the publication is spurious.

What was this 'best authority' which Wordsworth, and possibly Coleridge, had? Could they have received separate correspondence from Christian? We do not know, but John Adams, years later, when he was convinced he was safe from prosecution, also hinted that Christian had escaped from the island.

This version was given further credence by the fact that Peter Heywood, the former Midshipman on the *Bounty* and a man who knew Christian intimately, claimed to have seen him in Devonport.

Heywood, who had been pardoned and had risen to the rank of Captain, was walking in Fore Street and found himself behind a man whose shape, including the slightly bowed legs, so reminded him of Christian that he quickened his pace, at which the stranger turned, stared in shock and bolted. Heywood was convinced it was Christian.

If all this is true, it could indeed be that Christian recounted to Coleridge the story of his journey from Pitcairn to England and that this formed the basis or at least the inspiration for 'The Rime of the Ancient Mariner'.

But the most stunning possibility was the one put forward by the Australian adventurer and author, Becke, in his 1898 book, *The Mutineer.* Unlike some chroniclers of these events, Becke actually visited Pitcairn and gained the confidence of the islanders, who, he claimed, told him that 'in endeavouring to stop Christian from leaving Pitcairn, John Adams shot and killed him'.

This would, of course, account for the fact that the Pitcairners told so many differing stories: they were attempting to defend their patriarch!

One final, mind-boggling theory has recently been advanced by Dr. James Cerini of Kilmore East, Victoria, Australia. It will be recalled that John Adams signed aboard the *Bounty* as Alexander Smith. Dr. Cerini suggests that it may have been this man who died along with Mills, Martin and Brown, that Christian survived and seized the opportunity to hide his identity from possible future enforcers of Bligh's revenge. As Christian may have been the only person on Pitcairn who knew of Smith's real name, he could take this name without any of the others being aware that he was switching identities with someone they knew. Then years later, if need be, he could produce evidence to demonstrate that he, John Adams, was the relatively guiltless Smith. The majority on Pitcairn were children or Polynesians and may have known Adams by the name of Smith. The others could have been sworn to secrecy and this could explain why each eventually recounted a different story of Christian's fate. This, of course, would have required Christian to disguise his writing style and I must admit to being startled to find in Sydney's Mitchell Library, two totally different signatures, each attributed to Adams. If Christian did change his identity, this would also help to explain why, in the document handed to Captain Beechey, 'John Adams' described himself variously as 'I' and 'he'. Could the grey-haired patriarch who wrote that the mutiny was caused by 'Captain Bligh's disgusting behaviour' have been Fletcher Christian himself?

The hole in this theory is that Christian would have had to feign an abysmal ignorance of the English language and have had to

Left: Gustave Doré illustration for Coleridge's 'The Rime of the Ancient Mariner'
Above: John Adams

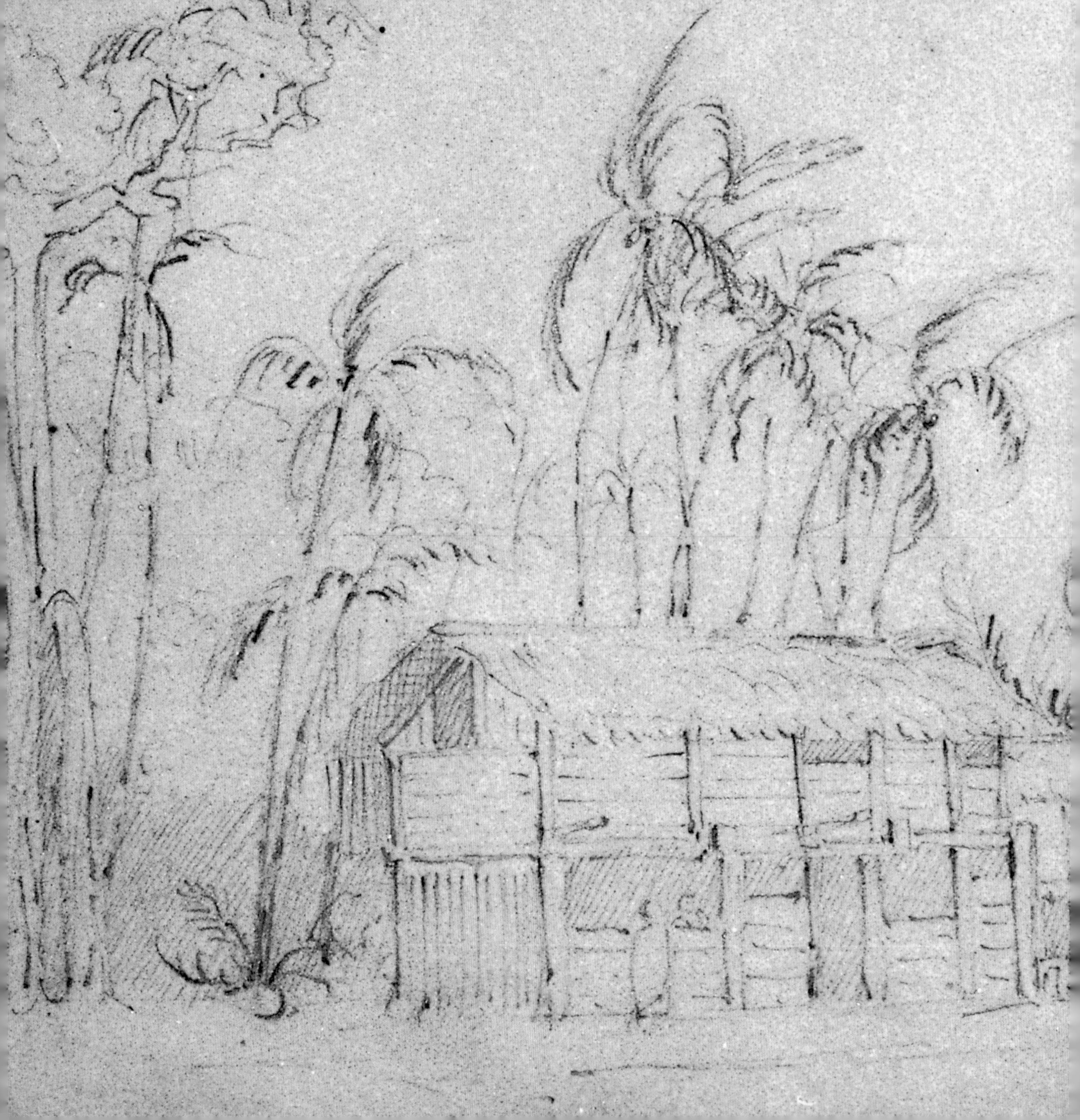

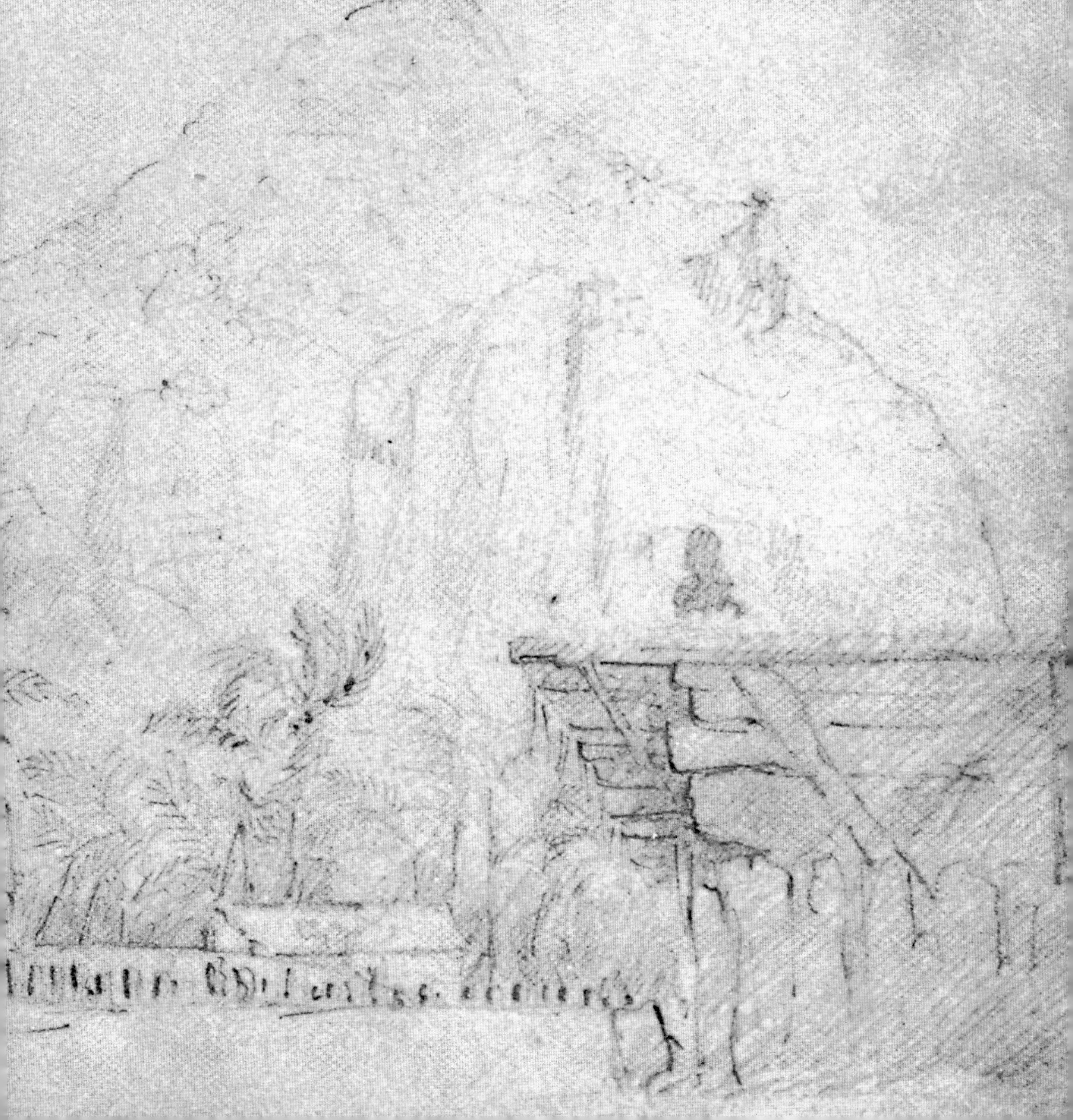

*Previous spread: View of Pitcairn
Below: Three signatures believed to
have been employed at various
times by John Adams, alias
Alexander Smith (alias Fletcher
Christian?)*

John Adams

John Adams.

John Adams

pretend to be learning it from Young (see next chapter). Despite the fascination of the various theories and legends, and although no grave has ever been found, I think we must assume that Christian died along with Williams, Mills, Martin and Brown.

The balance of events is well documented.

McCoy and Quintal escaped to the mountains whilst Young, being considered extremely handsome by the Tahitian women (perhaps because of his West Indian blood), was hidden by them from the wrath of their men.

Alexander Smith managed to elude his pursuers and returned to his house for supplies where he was fired at by the Polynesians. The musket ball passed through Smith's shoulder and out through his throat. Unused to firearms, the natives had consistently failed to despatch their victims by gunfire and had finished them off by the more traditional weapons of club or axe. This time, however, an attempt to deliver the *coup de grace* was made by using a musket at pointblank range. The gun was thrust into Smith's side – and twice misfired. Smith escaped, was recaptured and, through the intercession of the women, forgiven.

Fate, the gods or just plain luck had preserved Alexander Smith once again to play his crucial role in Pitcairn's future.

The four Polynesian men soon began quarrelling about the redistribution of the dead men's widows, and also cast envious eyes on the wives of some of the living. Whilst Young's wife, Susannah, was singing a song and being accompanied on the nose-flute by Teimua, one of her Polynesian admirers, a jealous countryman, Menallee, shot and killed him, and fled to the mountain refuge of McCoy and Quintal. The remaining two Europeans got a message to the two white outlaws that they would be welcome to return if they shot the murderer, Menallee, which they swiftly did but let it be known that they were unwilling to return while two natives still lived and were in control.

It was now the turn of the Tahitian women to conspire to murder, Bill Brown's widow lured the giant Toobouaian, Tetaheite, to bed and Young's wife then axed him across the throat as he lay sleeping. The first blow was insufficient to kill him and as he attempted to rise to his feet she split his skull open. This lady now signalled to Young, who shot the remaining native at point-blank range.

Of the 15 men who had landed at Pitcairn four years before, 11 had been murdered.

The survival of the community now seemed feasible until McCoy, who had once worked in a Scottish distillery, began extracting alcohol from the roots of the ti-tree, using the *Bounty*'s copper kettle as a still.†

From then on, McCoy and Quintal appear to have been in a continuous state of intoxication. In 1796, McCoy fastened a huge stone to his neck and hurled himself into the sea from the cliff below Christian's Cave. Quintal had gradually lost his mental stability and finally threatened to kill some children unless their mother‡ consented to live with him. For their own preservation, Smith and Young got him drunk, then executed him with an axe.

Now remaining, just nine years after the landing, were two men, eleven women and twenty children. Peace was on its way.

---

† *The kettle is today in the possession of the Norfolk Island Historical Society.*
‡ *Probably Young's wife*

CHAPTER 11

The Evangelisation of Pitcairn

Two adult men remained alive on Pitcairn – John Adams (alias Alexander Smith) and Edward Young.

Adams was a Cockney, an orphan, and had been brought up in the poorhouse. Young was well-educated and he spent many months helping to improve Adams's reading ability. The principal literature used for the reading lessons was the Bible and Prayer Book salvaged from the *Bounty*.

Young died of asthma (or possibly consumption) in 1800, and Adams filled his days with Bible reading and the drinking of spirits distilled from the juices of the ti-tree root. His libation was reputed to have been potent and his Bible-reading intensive. The result was that one night he had a hallucination in which the Archangel Michael attacked him with a dart. This brought about a total transformation in Adams. Overnight, he became fervently religious. And that undoubtedly saved the Pitcairn community from disintegration, if not annihilation.

Adams now took upon himself the task of educating four teenagers and nineteen children between the ages of seven and nine. The children looked upon him as teacher, religious instructor and father.

Though he has been described as 'a pious fraud'†, the result of his 20-year patriarchy was a community that visitors invariably described as idyllic.

Should it appear unlikely that a semi-literate seaman, whose drinking habits had not been totally cured by his 'visitation', should have wrought such a community from such a background, it must be remembered that all of his converts were Polynesian women and totally uneducated children.

Their lives were extremely simple. Subsistence farming and fishing occupied most of their daylight hours, interspersed with occasional recreational activities such as kite-flying, stilt-walking and a sport which they appear to have developed spontaneously – surfing. Captain Cook had reported that surfing was unknown even in Tahiti at that time

† *By Glynn Christian, in 'A Fragile Paradise'*

Far left: John Adams – J. A. Moerenhout, 1837
Left: John Adams's House, built by himself
Below: Church and Schoolhouse, Pitcairn

for the Lord's Day Morning

Suffer me not o Lord to waste
this Day in Sin or folly
But Let me worship thee with
much Delight teach me to know
more of thee and to Serve thee Better
than ever I have Done Before,
that I may Be fitter to Dwell
in heaven, where thy worship and
Service are everlasting Amen

John Adams

Above: John Adams's prayer

a keel, and went out on a rock and waited till a
large breaker came and when the top of it was
close to them, away they went with the piece of
wood under their belly on the top of this breaker
and directed themselves by their feet into the
little channel formed by the rocks, so that when
the surf left them they were only up to their
knees in water. They were very dexterous in
keeping off the rocks, which to us would be
inevitable death.

In 1806, Thursday October, aged 16, chose
a wife – Young's 31-years-old widow, Susannah
– and fathered the first of six sons. Susannah
was doubtless the murderer of the Toobouaian,
Tetaheite, but Thursday October could scarcely
have been aware of this as he must have been
about three at the time. Their marriage was
sealed with John Adams's ring (once Ned
Young's) and this became the custom for
generations of Pitcairners.†

Two years later, Pitcairn had her first
visitors. After landing her rum and gin at
Hobart Town (to Bligh's disgust), the *Topaz*
sailed north across the Pacific and chanced
across Pitcairn with no inkling that it was
inhabited.

In his log, Captain Folger wrote: 'I
discovered a boat paddling towards me'. It was a
Tahitian-style canoe containing three young
men 'as dark as natives' and almost naked.

The 'natives' yelled to them – in English!

A seaman called back that they were from
America.

"America? Is that in Ireland?"

'No – a long way from there. What is your
race?'

"We are Englishmen!"

'How can that be?'

"Because our father was an Englishman."

and, when he came across it in the Sandwich
Islands, he believed it to be unique.

The Pitcairners' name for it was 'sliding'
and Captain Raine later described the Pitcairn
surfboard as 'something resembling a butcher's
tray, but round at one end and square at the
other'. His Ship's Surgeon noted:

The islanders amused themselves by
taking a flat board about 3 feet long, on the
upper side smooth and on the under a ridge like

Left: H.M.S. 'Topaz' standing off Pitcairn

'Who is your father?'

"Aleck."

'Who is Aleck?'

"Don't you know Aleck?"

'How should we?'

"Well then, do you know Captain Bligh?"

Light dawned.

One of the young men was Friday October Christian.‡

Of the original mutineers, there was one single survivor, John Adams†, alias Alexander Smith. Adams was at first wary but when he learned that the visitors were American and not about to arrest him, he relaxed and begged for news of happenings in the outside world over the last two decades.

Folger told him of the French Revolution, the rise of Napoleon and the wars between England and France. When he recounted the

† *Recently the ring was unearthed by Mrs. H.E. Maude, wife of the distinguished historian, in an Adamstown garden and presented to Norfolk Island where, suitably mounted, it hangs in the Committee Room of the Legislative Assembly.*

‡ *Friday October changed his name to Thursday October, after eventually learning from a visiting sea-captain that his father had neglected to allow for the crossing of the date line!*

story of Nelson's illustrious victory at Trafalgar, ex-seadog Adams was deeply moved. 'He rose from his seat', wrote Folger, 'took off his hat, swung it three times round his head with three cheers, threw it on the ground sailor-like, and cried out: "Old England forever!"'

With this seemingly ancient patriarch (actually in his early forties) were four Tahitian women plus Fletcher's son and 23 children ranging from three years to 19. Of the 15 men who had arrived on the *Bounty*, 13 had died violent deaths. Yet the visiting sailors reported that the Pitcairners had become 'the world's most pious and perfect community'.

Captain Folger had discovered a race of 'Noble Savages', a race which would have thrilled Rousseau himself. The people were 'tall, robust, golden-limbed and good-natured of countenance'. All were extremely athletic and adept at surf-board riding.

They had an engaging simplicity based on unquestioning belief in a Divine Providence. Nobody (with the possible exception of Adams – it is not clear whether he excepted himself from the ban) drank alcohol. Nobody lied. Nobody stole. All worked for the common good. It is one of the great ironies of history that a legacy of mutiny and bloodshed had produced a model community.

Folger sent a copy of his log to the Admiralty in 1809 and, when this was ignored, personally wrote to them in 1813. Preoccupied with the activities of Napoleon, the authorities still chose to do nothing about punishing the sole survivor of a twenty-year-old mutiny. Moreover, they apparently disseminated this information to very few, possibly not even to Captain Bligh.

Seventeen years earlier, Bligh had read, in

Far right: Friday Fletcher October Christian – Lieut. J. Shillibeer of the 'Briton'

a publication called *The True Briton*, an account of a series of letters purported to have been received from Fletcher Christian, 'this extraordinary naval character', which related that the *Bounty*, following some lurid adventures, had been wrecked off the coast of Chile, and that Christian was now alive and well in Cadiz. On obtaining a copy of the letters, Bligh wrote to Sir Joseph Banks:

Mr Nicol has been so good as to send me down a pamphlet called Christian's Letters – is it possible that wretch can be at Cadiz and that he has had intercourse with his brother, that sixpenny Professor, who has more Law about him than honour – My Dear Sir, I can only say that I heartily despise the praise of any of the family of Christian, and I hope and trust yet that the mutineer will meet with his deserts.

However, Fletcher Christian's whereabouts had now taken such a low precedence on the scale of Britain's concerns that when the frigates *Targus* and *Briton* encountered the mutineer's descendants on Pitcairn in 1814, their captains, whom one might have expected to be well-informed by the Admiralty about events in this area, were as astonished as Folger had been. The log of Captain Pipon of the *Targus* reads:

As Pitcairn Island was described as uninhabited, we naturally conjected this in view could not be the place, particularly when, in bringing to, two or three miles off the shore, we observed the natives bring down their canoes on their shoulders, and shortly after darting through the heavy surf and paddling off to the ships; but our astonishment may be better conceived than decribed on finding that the inhabitants spoke the English language perfectly well.

Fletcher Christian's son came aboard and was described by Pipon as:

. . . a tall, fine young man about six feet high, with dark, black hair, and a countenance extremely open and interesting. He wore no clothes except a piece of cloth round his loins, a straw hat ornamented with black cock's feathers, and occasionally a peacock's, nearly similar to that worn by the Spaniards in South America, though smaller.

This extraordinary young man somehow had been instilled with the etiquette of hospitality, for he brought with him gifts including a whole hog. When the visitors went ashore they discovered that the island had hogs, goats and fowl in abundance as well as coconuts, yams, taro, figs, palm hearts and breadfruit, grown from the few kept on the *Bounty*. They were entranced with the village of Adamstown, perched on a rock platform high above the Landing Place and approached by scaling the Hill of Difficulty. The hub of the village was a grassy square, fringed with attractive wooden houses, those of Adams and Christian being of two stories. Attached to each house were hog and fowl pens, a bake-house and a a 'cloth-manufactury' wherein the bark of the mulberry tree was soaked in water and then beaten with wooden mallets.

The Pitcairners appeared to be extremely fit and strong. The men dressed in a vest and shorts (or simply wore a loin-cloth), the women in 'a loose bodice, with drapery reaching to their ankles, their long, black hair braided in a

† *Prior to joining 'Bounty', John Adams had deserted from another ship where he was known as 'Reckless Jack'. He signed on as Alexander Smith and reverted to his original name following the visit of the 'Targus'.*

Friday Fletcher October Christian

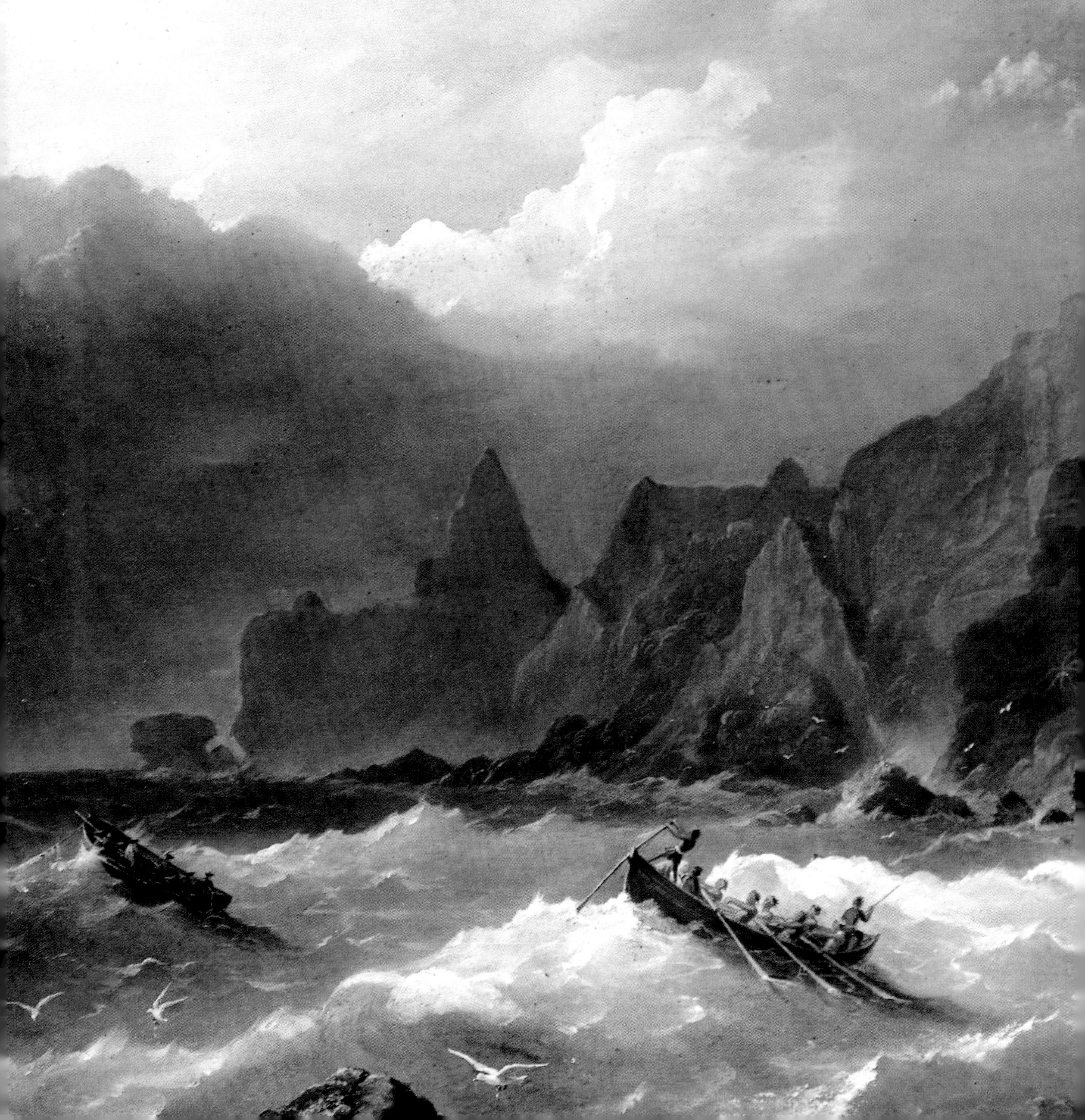

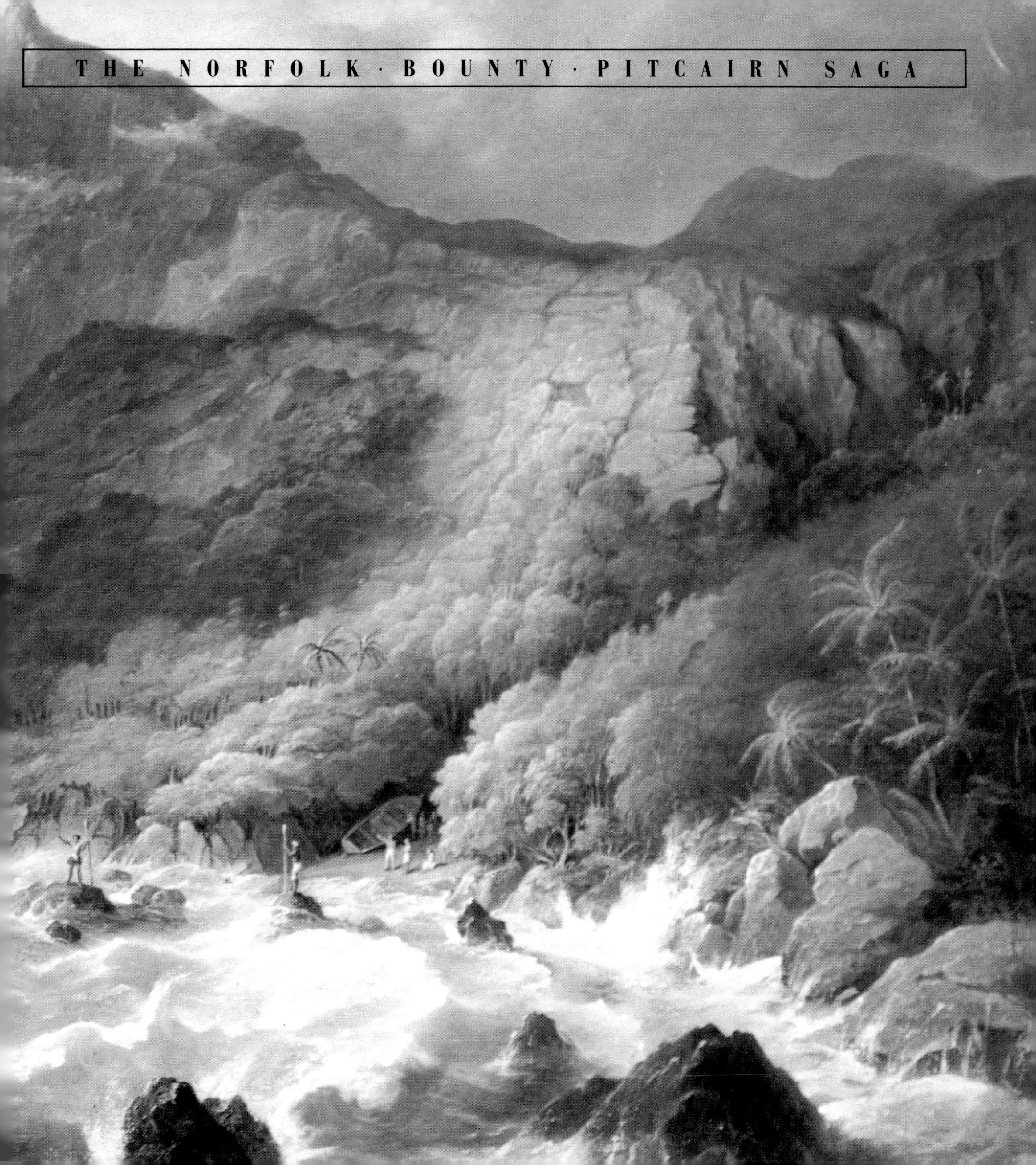

*Previous spread: 'Landing in
Bounty Bay' – F. W. Beechey
Above: 'Interior of house at
Pitcairn's Island' – W. E. Gordon*

knot at the back of the head and adorned with a
wreath of sweet-smelling flowers'. Even the men
smelled good, all using body fragrances made
from the oils of tropical flowers. The visitors
would have needed to be monsters to have
wrenched from this community their revered
mentor. As Captain Pipon recorded:

*In deed it would have been an act of great
cruelty and inhumanity to have taken him from
his family; who would have been left in the
greatest misery; and the settlement in all
probability annihilated.*

However, he covered his tracks by adding:

*. . . had we been inclined even to seize old†
Adams, it would have been impossible to have
conveyed him on board; again, to get to the
boats, we had to climb such precipices as were
scarcely accessible to any but goats and the
natives, and we had enough to do in holding on
by the different boughs and roots of trees, to
keep on our feet.*

The Captain added:

*. . . from the nature of the island, the
inhabitants might retire to such haunts as to
defy our utmost search; a measure which they
would naturally have had recourse to the
moment any intention of seizing any of them
had been manifested.*

Sir Thomas Staines, captain of the other
boat, *Briton*, was quick to note the natural
grace and singular lack of sophistication of the
Pitcairners, qualities which he believed gave
them great potential as catalysts in the
evangelisation of other Pacific people. He
recommended that they were 'well worth the
attention of our laudable religious societies,
especially that for propagating the Christian
religion; the whole of the inhabitants speaking
the Otahitian tongue as well as English'.

When *Briton* and *Targus* returned to
England and spread the word, the Pitcairners
became famous throughout the English-
speaking world.

The letter advising the Admiralty arrived
in 1815 and Bligh was alive for a further two
years, yet there is no documentation to be found
proving that he was ever informed of the
discovery. It would seem incredible that he
would not have heard the news then, even if he
had not when Folger first passed on his report,
yet in the extensive lore I can find no indication
that he did. What would have been his reaction?
Would he still have demanded the blood of
Adams? Following his Rum Rebellion court
martial, from which he emerged with his
reputation fairly intact, he had eventually been
made a Rear Admiral and lived in semi-
retirement during his final years. Perhaps, by
then, he had mellowed a little or, at least, had
priorities more important than the hunting

down of the last surviving mutineer. One would certainly like to think so.

Four years after Bligh's death, the *Surry* arrived at Pitcairn, her crew well aware of their responsibility to record accurate accounts of this intriguing race to add spice to the soirées of the British aristocracy and conviction to the hope of various religious groups that here were potential missionaries. The surgeon of the *Surry*, Dr David Ramsay, describes their landing in the ship's gig:

On our approaching the shore, the danger of landing through such a surf obliged us to lay on our oars till canoes which had got ahead of the breakers came up to us. Then we were quite enraptured, the mountainous height of the land, the abrupt precipices, the roaring surf and the coppered natives on the black rocks, their fairy forms now seen, now hid by the dashing wave, seemed the genii in the fancied regions of Alladin. But we were afraid to land as there is no beach and the breakers running high, we waited till the men in the canoes came up with us and they should show us the way to get ashore. The channel formed by large rocks being very narrow, it requires great caution in the surf. One man, Quintal, swam out to us to watch the signal and tell us when to pull in, another stood on a high rock with a branch to wave to him, the rest stood on each side of the rocks showing the passage through which the boat must go.

The man on the rock seeing the sea smooth gave the signal and in we went. When we came to the men on the rocks they took hold of the boat and ran her slap out of the surf and then took her (all of us having got out) on their shoulders and carried her up into the shade.

After this, we made ready to go to their

houses, which were about 100 feet above the level of the sea and about half a mile to the north of the landing place – the road was very difficult of ascent to us but we all got up safe – at an open space about half way to the houses they stopped and said prayers – they first sing a psalm then pray (on their knees) then sing a psalm again which concludes their services. I have never at any time seen a more serious manner in devotion than at this time. It is a lesson to the most austere Christian in Europe.

We were welcomed on our arrival at the village, if I may call it so, by all the people as if we were their brothers or children.

Throughout the stay of the *Surry*, the Pitcairners demonstrated an innocence and a conviction which made a sham of the religious posturings of most of the rest of the world:

Dr Ramsay made careful notes of their speech:

No good in doing wrong ... When I do wrong something in my head tell me so. Suppose one man strikes me, I no strike again, for the Book say 'suppose one man strike you on one side, turn the other to him' ... suppose he bad man strike me, I no strike him, because no good that, suppose he kill me, he can't kill my soul. He no can grasp that, that he go to God much better place than here.

Money no good to us, if you give me money, I throw it in the sea.

If it appeared that Satan had finally been vanquished in Pitcairn, back in the temporary Eden of Norfolk he was stirring once more.

† *Adams was 50 at the time but apparently had the demeanour of a man much older.*

Next spread: 'View of houses, Pitcairn' – W. E. Gordon

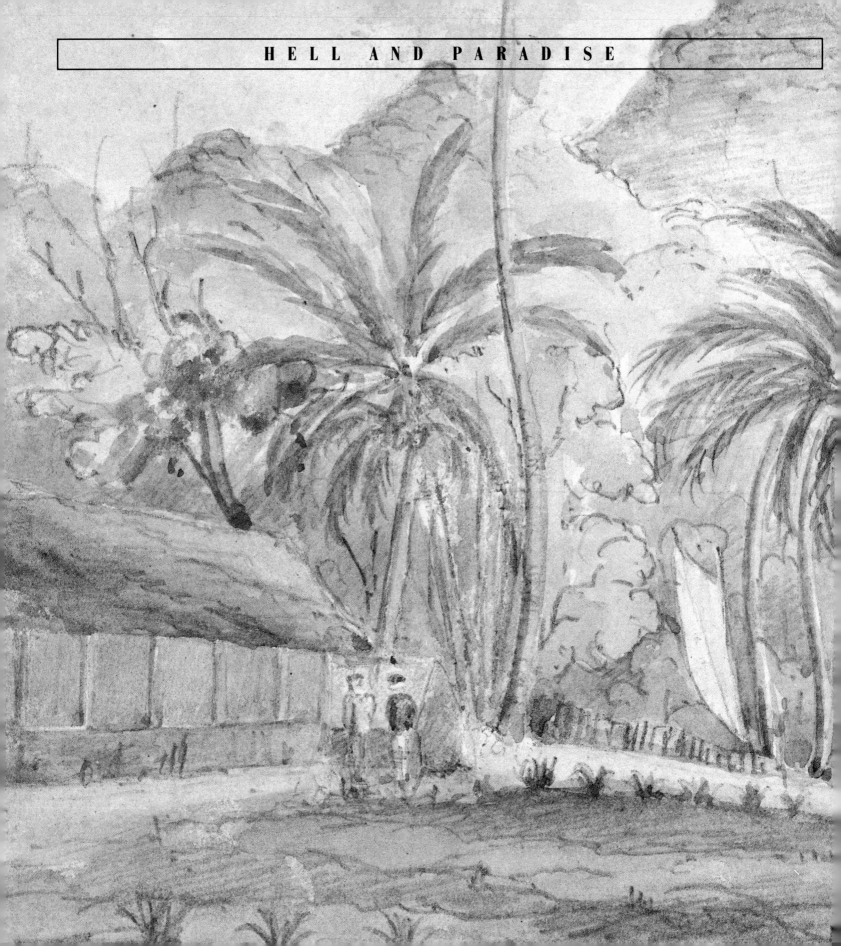

CHAPTER 12

Second Settlement – Norfolk

After 11 years of drowsing in the sun, Norfolk Island was elected by His Majesty's Government to be the site of another penal colony.

The original settlement had been established primarily in order to develop the resources of the island. This one had no such purpose. As the gaols of New South Wales and Van Diemen's Land were overflowing with bushrangers and other doubly convicted criminals, the Second Settlement, as it was euphemistically described, was designed to be conducted along the lines of 'a great Hulk or Penitentiary' . . . for the incarceration of 'colonially re-convicted incorrigibles'.

It was designated to become 'a place of the severest punishment short of death'. Sir Thomas Brisbane wrote: 'I could wish it to be understood that the felon who is sent there is forever excluded from hope of return'.

Captain Turton's landing party discovered that the settlement had become completely overgrown. Not one of the dozen dogs left on the abandoned island to 'destroy the pigs' was left alive, but pigs in abundance were happily scrabbling in the tumbled ruins.

The 57 convicts were swiftly put to work constructing stone walls to shut them out from life and gallows to blot them out from it forever. The gaol, used to no recent sound but the murmuring of the waves, was soon to hear again its theme-song – the high-pitched wail of the lash.

Turton was swiftly succeeded (in December 1825) by Captain Vance Donaldson who brought with him orders from the new Governor of New South Wales, General Sir Ralph Darling, that all women, whether bond or free, were to be withdrawn from the island on the next vessel, so as not to be tainted by the depraved and dissolute men which it had been designed to hold.

To avoid deportation, one woman fled to the bush with her three children, only to be

Far left: J. T. Morisset as an Ensign, either painted before his disfigurement or idealised by the artist
Left: Two medals of Captain Morisset
Below: The Pentagonal Prison, Kingston

forced back by their wails of hunger. Neither she, nor any other of the thirty women, was allowed to stay.

Shortly after, Donaldson was faced with a mass breakout. A group of about thirty convicts, led by a certain Black John Goff, overpowered their overseers, stole three small boats, stove in the one remaining in the boatshed and rowed to Phillip Island. Most of them were soon captured, except for Black John, who, though mad with thirst, eluded capture for days. His final refuge was the summit of an awesome, 1000-foot peak where they at last hunted him down. Somehow this story became grafted on to one about a latter-day convict, the notorious 'Jacky-Jacky' Westwood. Legend has it that he jumped from this peak to his death. Though this is quite untrue†, the peak is called Jacky Jacky to this day and a huge shadow on the north cliff of Phillip Island, which in certain lights seems to coalesce into the silhouette of a man, is known as Jacky Jacky's Ghost.

It is said that Emily Bay, one of the most enchanting inlets in the world, was named after the wife of one of the Second Settlement's most

hideous commandants, known to the prisoners as Lasher Morisset.

Morisset had demonstrated his taste for killing in the war against Napoleon in Egypt and in the Peninsular War where he earned a medal bearing seven clasps. At either Albuera or Talavera he received a sabre cut which disfigured him for life. His face was horribly scarred, and apparently so was his mind. His sadism was rivalled by only one other commandant, John Price, of whom more later.

Morisset's first request to the British Government was for a treadmill which was to employ 30 men and 20 women and 'to instill discipline into these incorrigible felons'. The island already possessed a crank mill, but Morisset apparently considered it insufficiently ghastly. It operated on the principle of a capstan but was appallingly heavy, its team of convicts being required to turn two gigantic grindstones. The overseer sat in a gallery high up in the wall, ignoring the screeches, curses and hoots of the toiling wretches below him but making sure that no man flagged for an instant. It is said that the fearful clankings and grindings of the crank mill could be heard as far away as Anson Bay.

Morisset's request for a treadmill was refused, not on the grounds that it was too inhumane, but because it was considered too costly.

He had other ways. Permanent ballast in his gig were a triangle and two scourgers poised to administer instant justice at Morisset's whim. When he judged a flogging to be insufficiently brutal, Morisset delighted in applying the lash in person.

In a letter to the Secretary of State for the Colonies, an observer wrote:

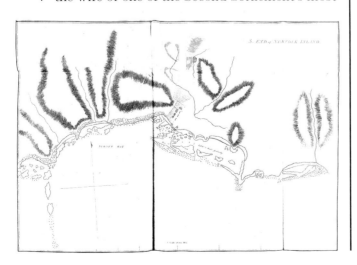

If the wretches at Norfolk Island were fiends and not men, they could not be worse treated. There is no parallel to the cruelties practised on them. I beg to observe, my Lord, that in the report of Mr. Commissioner Bigge he notices that he examined the backs of prisoners at Newcastle and found them knotted and furrowed in consequence of severe scourging. That scourging was inflicted by Colonel Morisset, the present Commandant at Norfolk Island who is, save for the late Captain Logan of Moreton Bay, one of the most improper that could have been selected.

Judge Sir Roger Therry wrote of a group of convicts sent to Sydney by Morisset to give evidence at the trial of one of their brethren:

Their sunken glazed eyes, deadly pale faces, hollow fleshless cheeks and once manly limbs shrivelled and withered up a if by premature old age, created horror among those in court. There was not one of the six who had not undergone from time to time, a thousand lashes each and more. They looked less like human beings than the shadows of gnomes who had risen from their sepulchral abode. What man was or ever could be reclaimed under such a system as this?

When reports like this were ignored by Morisset's superiors, he was encouraged to indulge in even more atrocious acts. Deciding that convicts were wasting time by picking oranges when they should have been at hard labour, Morisset ordered that every orange tree on the island should be cut down.

Such depravities are destined to culminate in rebellion and, in January, 1834, almost the entire convict force endeavoured to throw off their chains. The plan was to capture Morisset and 'cut him up into four pieces to be divided

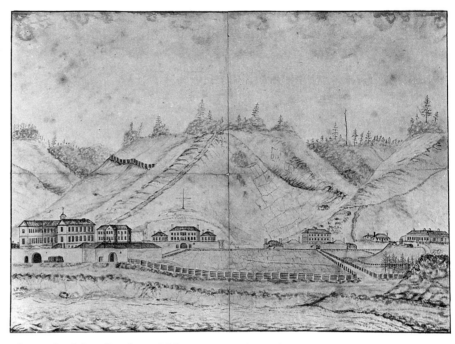

Far left: South end of Norfolk Island
Above: The Settlement in 1838

about the island'. The rabble were cut down by musket fire and those who thus died were the lucky ones. 162 were gaoled, many on the advice of informers, any offering the slightest defence being given between 100 and 300 lashes each under the direction of Morisset's able lieutenant, Captain 'Flogger' Fyans.

Morisset was removed from his post but the process of justice continued on its relentless course. Major Anderson arrived in April with orders that 55 of the mutineers were to face trial. 'Public Affairs' kept the mainland judge busy for six months so for this entire time all 55 were chained to ring-bolts in their cells.

Their defending lawyer said:

These men, not one above 35 years of age, were grey, wizened and shrunken, their eyes dull and unseeing, the skin stretched taut on the

† *See Chapter 15.*

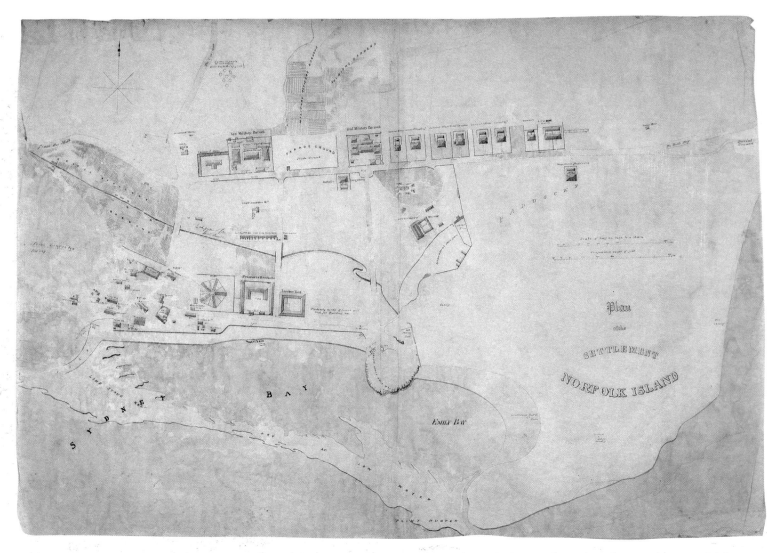

Above: Plan of the Settlement, 1844
Far right: Barney Duffy's Pine –
from a 1904 postcard

cheeks; they spoke in whispers and were awful to behold.

Judge Burton, however, was unmoved. He described the men as 'a Cage full of Unclean Birds, full of Crimes against God and Man, Murders and Blasphemies and all Uncleanness'.

Some of the 29 men convicted to die begged His Honour to allow a 'man of the cloth' to visit them. The priest, later to become Bishop Ullathorne, wrote in his autobiography:

I have to record the most heart-rending scene that I ever witnessed. The turnkey unlocked the cell door and . . . then came forth a yellow exhalation, the produce of the bodies of the men confined therein. I announced to them who were reprieved from death and which of them were to die. It is a literal fact that each man who heard his reprieve wept bitterly; and each man who heard his condemnation of death went down on his knees and, with dry eyes, thanked God they were to be delivered from this horid place.

The morning came, they received on their knees the sentence as the will of God. Loosened from their chains, they fell down in the dust, and, in the warmth of their gratitude, kissed the very feet that had brought them peace.

Those remaining alive were discouraged from complaining of any sickness because of the inevitable charge of 'malingering'. Nevertheless, many desperately ill men and women climbed the thoughtlessly steep steps to the Civil Hospital, where, likely as not, they would have their meagre rations stolen by the so-called surgeons, to be fed to their fowls and pigs.

The standard treatment for consumption was a mustard plaster. For tetanus or infected burns, the surgeons would pack hot manure around the wound.

Amputations were performed without anaesthetic and cauterised with a hot iron or boiling tar.

Legend has it that a man called Barney Duffy escaped from this travesty of a hospital and miraculously remained at large for seven years. During all of this time, he is said to have lived in a giant hollow pine.

Barney was finally caught, goes the legend, by three troopers – Turner, Heffernan and Warnham. As they were clapping him in manacles, the giant, long-haired convict screamed a curse at them: 'Take me . . . ye red-coated, lily-livered lice! Aye! And then I'll hang – but hear my curse on ye: So surely as ye do this, before me corpse has hung a week on King's Town gallows, ye'll meet a violent death!'

Two days after the hanging, his captors were fishing off Headstone Point when all three were swept off the rocks to their deaths.

Previous writers have insisted that this story is apocryphal on the grounds that no trace of a prisoner of that name can be found in the records. No trace of a *free* man of this name can be found in the records either, yet close to the spot is an area known as 'Barney Duffy's Gulley'. This was shown on a map prepared under the direction of the House of Commons and published by J. Arrowsmith in 1882.

The hollow tree certainly existed and was reverently pointed out to visitors by the locals up until the Fifties when it was destroyed by fire – it is said by an arsonist.

Charles Turner's body was found and his gravestone is still to be seen in the cemetery. The other two were never seen again but a memorial to them stands at Headstone.

The flaw in the evidence is that the gulley was charted in 1841 but the drownings did not occur until 1850. Could Barney have possibly stayed at large for over a decade? Or was he a free man who worked in this gulley before committing a crime and becoming a convict?

Another story that is hard to prove – or disprove – is the Legend of Bloody Bridge. This is how it was told to me:

Here, in the time of Major Anderson, the merciless, one-eyed Scot they called 'Potato Joe' for his act of substituting potatoes for bread in the convict's rations, a labour gang was constructing this beautifully-designed bridge. (One of the ironies of Norfolk is that all the buildings are designed with a remarkable eye for timeless grace, a refinement doubtless lost on the poor devils who built them.)

The convicts' every step was impeded by irons, mostly weighing 15 pounds and some as much as 22 pounds. Dysentery constantly gnawed at their vitals. Already half-crazed by their suffering, they were goaded ceaselessly by their overseer in the hope of inducing a glance of protest. This offence, called 'dumb insolence', earned immediate retribution – the cat-o'-nine-tails.

Suddenly, one of them exploded and drove a pick through the brain of his tormentor.

Knowing that every one of them would be punished horribly, the gang walled up the bleeding corpse in the bridge. When the overseer's relief turned up at midday, he asked where his predecessor was. 'Oh,' was the reply, 'he went for a swim down there in the bay. We think he must have drowned.'

Right: Lieutenant-Colonel Joseph Anderson

Unfortunately for them, through the still-wet mortar between the bluestones, something began to ooze . . . (At this point, the raconteur pointed dramatically and one was almost convinced that one could see a dark red stain) . . . *It was the blood of the walled-up overseer!*

In the realm of the unproven, one final tale:

Old islanders say that opposite Rawson Hall was a guardhouse containing a prison cell, 20 feet by 14 feet, completely devoid of doors or windows. Prisoners were taken up a stone stairway to its roof and lowered down into the pitch-black, there to be confined for days or weeks.

On a wall of this dungeon, they say, was the signature of Rufus Dawes!†

As the walls have long since been plastered over, the story can never be verified.

† *Hero of 'For the Term of His Natural Life'*

CHAPTER 13

Fresh Blood

On 10th December, 1823, the British whaler, *Cyrus*, arrived at Pitcairn bearing two men who were to introduce to the island its first (and almost its last) non-*Bounty*, non-Polynesian blood.

As John Adams's wife, Teio, whom he called Mary, was now blind, Adams was finding it difficult to care for her and simultaneously cope with the teaching of an ever-increasing horde of children. Upon his request, Captain John Hall agreed to allow one of his complement to remain on Pitcairn in the role of school-teacher. This was John Buffett, a man with a remarkable history of survival.

He had survived ferocious storms in Manila Bay and the Moluccas. He had been shipwrecked in the Bay of St. Lawrence, witnessing the death of 42 souls, then shipwrecked again south of Boston. In manner, however, this adventure-toughened seadog appears to have come across as a mild, soft-spoken scholar.

His friend, John Evans, was not invited to stay but jumped ship and hid in a tree until *Cyrus* sailed.

Buffett wasted little time in finding a female companion and, just nine weeks later, married Dolly Young, who produced a lightish-skinned offspring on 13th January, 1925 [1825]. Evans chose Adams's daughter, Rachel, married her on 26th November, 1924 [1824], and presented old

John Adams with a granddaughter the following year.

Through all the ships' visits since 1808, Adams had steadfastly denied any complicity in the mutiny. But by the time the warship H.M.S. *Blossom* arrived in 1825 he was 62 years old and at last convinced that the Admiralty had no intention of prosecuting him. Wearing his finest regalia – a sailor's shirt and trousers – and carrying a low-crowned hat, he put off in a boat with a welcoming party of ten of his 'subjects'.

The old man handed to Captain Beechey an account of the mutiny – a strange document

Far left: George Hunn Nobbs as Chaplain of Pitcairn Island
Left: Pitcairn Island – Smyth (of H.M.S. 'Blossom'), 1825
Below: Facsimile of signed document handed to Captain Beechey by John Adams

in which he sometimes refers to himself in the first person and sometimes in the third. In it he claimed that the mutiny came about through 'the seduction of Tahiti' and 'the disgusting behaviour of Captain Bligh'.

The other Pitcairners who came aboard the *Blossom* bombarded the crew with questions. Beechey wrote:

Having no latches on their doors, they were ignorant of the manner of opening ours and we were consequently attacked on all sides with 'Please may I sit down or get up or go out of the cabin or please to open or shut the door'. Not using surnames themselves, they quickly learned the first name of every officer on the ship. Whenever similarity to their own name occurred, they attached themselves to that person as a matter of course.

The newcomers were taken ashore in the islanders' boat, two at a time, arriving much relieved to have made the ferocious passage unscathed. They were treated to an island hog-feast, the animal being wrapped in ti-tree leaves and cooked in a ground oven, Tahitian-style. The women were obliged to wait until the men had finished before they could eat, an imposition they accepted cheerfully on the grounds that 'as Man was made first, he should be served first'.

Below: 'Interior of Pitcairn Island' – by Captain Beechey

Close to the village, Beechey was intrigued with a giant banyan tree. He paced out its circumference and recorded it as 200 paces.

Some of the *Blossom*'s crew were taken down 'The Rope', and shown some ancient stone axes and some primitive drawings cut into the rocky cliff face. A later visitor described these as 'rude outline figures of three men, of the sun, and a little sun, of the moon in two phases, four stars, a bird, a straight line placed in a slanting position, resemblances to our letters *e,i,j,l*, to a moon having a star in it, the numeral 5, and something like the handle of a whip, whose lash is turned back and tied in the centre'.†

On a lofty peak overlooking Bounty Bay, four stone carvings were found, hewn out of a piece of red lava. They were not unlike those on Easter Island.

Before leaving, Beechey officially married Adams to his blind wife, Teio. The patriarch told the captain that he feared the island was becoming overcrowded, and extracted a promise from him that he would seek the help of the British Government in finding another island home for the endangered flock, 'in N.S. Wales or Van Diemen's Land, or some place where they can all settle together and cultivate the ground or labour as may be required'. It is far from certain whether this was the wish of the majority, but Beechey duly passed on the request.

In the meantime, John Buffett began conducting most of the religious services and gradually began to usurp the position of spiritual leader.

But the water of the font of religion itself can occasionally be whipped into frenzy for, in 1828, in the month after which he had been named, Thursday October was surprised to learn that his daughter, Mary, one of Buffett's pupils, had produced an offspring sired by her tutor. Buffett was apparently forgiven this misdemeanour and continued for some time in his role of principal purveyor of literacy and divinity.

† *'The Bounty and After' by Albert Hazzard*

Left: 'Young Pitcairn Man' – Smyth (of H.M.S. 'Blossom')
Above: Pitcairn idol resembling a human figure – Otago Museum

Right: Hannah Young née Adams

However, a few weeks after the birth, a small ship was spotted approaching the island. In it was the 29-years-old George Hunn Nobbs, a former privateer and soldier-of-fortune who was eventually to oust both Buffett and Adams and become pastor to the Pitcairn flock for an astonishing 55 years. He was accompanied by a large, black-bearded, mysterious American called Noah Bunker. Nobbs's story was that he had come to an agreement with Bunker in South America whereby he would refit Bunker's 20-ton boat at a cost of £150 on the condition that the latter should accompany him to Pitcairn Island. Bunker was extremely ill on arrival and asked to see the captain of a visiting ship, the *Volador*.†

The *Volador*'s captain was the Belgian Antoine Moerenhout, a remarkable adventurer, a talented writer and illustrator, and a humanitarian rare for his time. He called frequently on Pitcairn and became to the islanders a friend, guide and protector for many years.

Moerenhout went with Nobbs to see Bunker and later wrote, in his *Voyages aux Iles du Grand Ocean:*

I saw a man lying on a mattress which partly covered the floor. Near him was a woman who was waving small branches to chase away the flies. At my approach, the sick man signalled to me with his left hand for me to sit down.

His appearance contained something sinister. He was a man about thirty five years old, with black beard and hair, thin and very pale face, a covered forehead, very large eyes and thick eyebrows, and upon his features, extraordinary in their entirety; could be read at the same time suffering and an unusual exaltation of spirit, which, while despairing of life, knew how to struggle against sorrow.

The Pitcairners were disturbed by the presence of these two misfits but allowed them to stay on until Bunker should recover. Nobbs took this opportunity to ingratiate himself with the locals. He claimed that he was appalled by the vice and lack of Christianity in the outside world and wanted nothing more than to instruct the new generation in the ways of grace and piety. Soon, he was accepted by all but the man whose prestige he was eroding, John Buffett.

Buffett also may have had some hints from Bunker about Nobbs's less than impeccable former life, but he could not have imagined the half of it.

Nobbs was born the illegitimate son of Jemima ffrench, wife of Francis Rawdon-Hastings, first Marquis of Hastings and second Earl of Moira. He claimed that at an early age he was moved from Ireland to England and adopted the name of the family who brought him up until the age of 14 when he took service on H.M.S. *Indefatigable*. He professed to be ashamed of his illegitimacy but must have been proud of his noble antecedence as, on occasions, he signed his name as 'Rawdon'. He called his Norfolk home 'Moira' and named his fourth child after his mother. Several of his grandchildren were named Rawdon, Hastings and ffrench and the latter name, so alien to the Pacific, survives on Norfolk to this day.

Nobbs had an early taste of hypocrisy and inhumanity when he sailed to New South Wales on a vessel carrying 198 convicts below decks. In 1816, he joined a warship as a mercenary to fight the Spanish in South America. Over a year and a half, the privateer captured several ships

Left: Hannah Adams and baby

and sank others. Nobbs was captured by the Spanish and became a virtual slave working on the fortifications of the Port of Callao. He managed to bribe his way to freedom and rejoin

† *'Volador' is Spanish for Flying Fish. She was apparently well named as she was so shallow-gutted that her sails, it was said, 'spent as much time under water as above it'.*

his ship which happened to be less than a hundred miles away up the coast. It sailed to Manila where it plundered a rich Spanish merchant ship, earning Nobbs the substantial reward of two thousand dollars and enabling him to become master of his own privateer.

In Chile, he was taken prisoner by the Indian troops of a Spanish Royalist but freed by the rebels. Joining the Chilean Navy, he found himself in a party endeavouring to recapture some British property from the Royalists. They were ambushed and 48 of the 64 killed or wounded. The dead and dying were hurled into a nearby river and the remainder shot, four at a time. When only Nobbs and three others were left, they were exchanged for some Royalist officers.

Following many more harrowing adventures, Nobbs grew tired of the brutality of

his life-style and returned home where he was reunited with his mother as she lay dying. Legend suggests that he had something of an Oedipus complex and at his mother's request that 'her wrongs and his' should be buried in some remote spot, he sailed to South America where he persuaded Bunker to transport him to a place where violence was unknown.

No amount of research has been able to pierce the veil that has shrouded Bunker, but it would seem that he was even more in need of balm for his soul than was Nobbs. He could not shake himself out of a peculiarly fatalistic gloom, a state which could well have been the result of drug-taking. He made many attempts at suicide. Several times he tried poison and one night he threw himself off a cliff. A fall of two hundred feet having failed to kill him, he asked a child for a knife but was refused.

Finally he took an overdose of laudanum, lay in a coma for 28 hours, regained consciousness for five minutes and died without uttering a word to throw light on his motivation.

Shortly afterwards, John Adams caught a fever and Nobbs swiftly stepped into the breech. His stepfather, Isaac Nobbs, was a missionary and it was from him that George absorbed, along with a fascination for the Pacific, a familiarity with Anglican ritual.

Moerenhout learned that there were to be two separate Sunday services, one conducted by Buffett and one by Nobbs. He wrote:

I was very surprised to see that now they were going to hold services in two different places; and it was not long before I gathered that George Nobbs had already succeeded in making a split among these people who, before his arrival, had lived together in harmony. After a few minutes, Nobbs began the service by

Previous spread: Pitcairn view, 1833
Right: Sketch of John Adams by Captain Beechey, a few years before Adams's death

118

reading several passages from the Bible: then some hymns were sung. After these he gave a long sermon, which sent Mr. Brock to sleep, although the sermon was fairly good and well delivered. The service ended with a special prayer, the principal fault of which was that it included too many things; but when he was praying for old Adams, there were tears in every eye.

Although George Hunn Nobbs was eventually to become a revered figure in the community, there were many beside the shrewd and humane Moerenhout who at this stage doubted his motives.

Back at the Admiralty, Sir John Barrow received despatches from visiting ships questioning Nobbs's credentials and was driven to an unusual degree of vehemance in writing:

This Nobbs is probably one of those half-witted persons who fancy they have received a 'call' to preach nonsense – some cobbler escaped from his stall, or tailor from his shopboard. Kitty Quintal's cant phrase – 'we want food for our souls', and praying at meals for 'spiritual nourishment', smack not a little of the jargon of the inferior caste of evangelicals. (Barrow was referring to Quintal's remark to Captain Waldegrave in 1836 which was the subject of many a pious sermon in Britain. On being told that the ship's chaplain was coming ashore to lead them in prayer, she cried: 'God bless you! God bless you! Will he stay with us?' "I cannot spare him," replied the captain, "he is the clergyman on my ship. I have brought you some clothes, which King George sends you." 'We would rather have food for our souls', averred the woman.)

Barrow continued:

Whoever this pastoral drone may be, it is but too evident that the preservation of the innocence, simplicity, and happiness of these amiable people is intimately connected with his speedy removal from the island.

In this rare instance, history was to prove 'Barrow of the Admiralty' to be wrong.

On the 5th of March, 1829, John Adams died, aged 62, and was followed nine days later by his blind wife, Teio. Of the original 25 'mutineers', he had survived the longest. Eight had been murdered, Thompson and Churchill on Tahiti, the other six on Pitcairn. Quintal had committed suicide, four had drowned wearing irons when the *Pandora* sank, and three had been hanged. Those who died violently had an average age of 27. Seven were either acquitted or pardoned and one of these, Peter Heywood, died an Admiral. But John Adams outlived them all.

Following his death, Nobbs gradually increased his influence whilst Buffett's band of supporters diminished.

And now benign bureaucracy took a hand . . .

*Bottom: John Adams's grave
Below: John Adams's tombstone –
National Maritime Museum,
England*

CHAPTER 14

Seduction of the Innocents

Captain Beechey, true to his word, conveyed to the authorities John Adams's fears that the Pitcairners were beginning to outgrow their island. He also informed various religious groups that these bilingual innocents could prove very useful in aiding the missionaries in their endeavours to save the souls of the Tahitians.

The Tahitians were receptive to the idea for other reasons. The decision of a meeting held between their chiefs and Commander Laws, representing H.M. Government, was translated as follows:

. . . We want an officer, a consul, at Tahiti, as representative of the King of Great Britain, that he may assist us: it is of no use depending on the consul at the Sandwich Islands; we have long known that we can obtain no advantage from him. We wish much that a British ship of war would come frequently to Tahiti, to take away to their own land those bad foreigners who trouble us.

We wish to do our duty towards the Britons. You are powerful and rich, but we are weak children —

On behalf of Pomare Waheine, the administrator of the Regency;
APAAPA, Secretary of State

TEPAU, Judge
ARUPAEO, Governor and Judge
TEPOEA, One of the Seven Supreme Judges
MARE, a District Judge

In 1829, the Reverend Nott nurtured visions of removing the Pitcairners from their homeland but eventually relented and advised the London Missionary Society that the masters of several visiting vessels had reported that the islanders were perfectly happy and had no wish to leave the island. However, a missionary named Crook(!) convinced the Governor of New South Wales otherwise and in 1831 the Pitcairners were surprised to discover a ship on their doorstep, sent with the intention of transporting them to Tahiti. Within four days, all 87 of them, with an average age of 17, had been convinced of the joys awaiting them, had

Far left: George and Hannah Young – M. Albert-Montemont, Collection de Voyages Modernes
Above left: John Adams with children near his house – Smyth (of H.M.S. 'Blossom')
Above: Pomare Waheine
Below: 'Near the mouth of Whapiano river, island of Otahytey', 1792 – G. Tobin

packed up, and been herded on to the *Lucy Ann* which, escorted by H.M.S. *Comet*, headed back to the land that had so entranced their forebears.

When the *Lucy Ann* docked at Papeete, 50 Tahitian women came on board and shocked the Pitcairners with their licentious behaviour. The very next morning the newcomers demanded to be taken home. This was refused and they were moved into houses shared by Tahitians, an idea which the missionaries believed would assist in de-heathenising the pagans. All but three of the Pitcairners had Tahitian blood in their veins but they had all been purified (or brainwashed, according to one's point of view) for generations, and the nightly 'orgies' they were forced to witness disgusted them.

A dreadful fever now attacked these people who were, until then, amongst the healthiest people on earth. The first to die was the oldest, Fletcher Christian's son, Thursday October. He was followed by the youngest, the baby Lucy Ann Quintal. Ten more died in the space of two months. After twenty weeks, the authorities had to admit failure and the survivors were allowed to return to their beloved homeland.

The old friend of the Pitcairners, Captain Moerenhout, offered one of his pearling schooners and John Buffett led an advance party to prepare the way for a mass return.

The captain of the sloop *Zebra* then wrote to the Governor of New South Wales:

As no direct Communication can have reached your Excellency respecting the Pitcairns People, I beg to inform you that, although every possible attention and kindness was shewn to them by the Queen (Pomare), the Chiefs and the Tahitians in general, and although every want was amply provided by the Agent appointed to supply them, they became wretched and melancholy, and pined so much after their Native Island, that, after five Months' residence here during which period twelve of their Number died, the Missionaries, with that Christian feeling which marks their Character, raised a subscription of six hundred and fifty Spanish Dollars, and Chartered a Vessel which took them to Pitcairn's Island in September last.

Despite the good offices of the missionaries, the Pitcairners were required to subsidise the cost of their return journey with the last of the possessions brought from their home, including their blankets and even the last of the bronze bolts from the *Bounty.*

They arrived at Pitcairn just in time to prevent it being annexed by the French, a fate which Norfolk Island had narrowly escaped 44 years earlier. During their absence, their houses had been broken into by natives from Bora Bora and their hogs had run wild, destroying their crops. The Tahitian fever continued to stalk them and another five succumbed, including their leader, Edward Young.

Into this demoralised community now came an extraordinary charlatan named Joshua Hill, styling himself variously 'Captain Hill' or 'Lord Hill'.

He arrived on the 29th October on the barque *Pomare* and announced that he had been sent by the British Government to become their new pastor and to 'adjust the internal affairs of the island'. If any islanders did not obey his commands, he announced, he had only to send word to the British consul in Valparaiso and a force would be sent forthwith to punish them.

Following a grand tour of the island, he selected the best-looking house, commandeered a room for his personal use, and informed the owner that he was privileged to be so selected. So arrogant and audacious was Hill, and so naive were the Pitcairners – so willing to believe that 'people don't tell lies' – that they took him at face value. But the Belgian sea-captain, Moerenhout, as ever the protector of these young innocents, swiftly summed up the newcomer.

Hill, he wrote, 'exhibited a puerile vanity: a bombastic pride: a dangerous fanaticism: and an implacable hatred of anyone who dared to oppose his plans in any way whatever'.

Hill cared little for the opinions of a seafarer who would be on the island only infrequently. He moved swiftly to stamp out the intemperance which some of the islanders had brought back with them from Tahiti and imposed strict book censorship: 'All books coming on shore must undergo my inspection and such as I condemn must be burned by the common hangman'. A prison was then built in which Hill threatened to incarcerate anyone who broke his laws.

In an amazingly short space of time, he was ready to introduce the weapon with which so many dictators have divided, then enslaved, their subjects: xenophobia. Fulminating against his perceived rivals Nobbs, Buffett and Evans, this latest arrival announced: 'I will cause the first captain of a man-of-war who arrives to remove these lousy foreigners from the island'. The docility with which George Hunn Nobbs accepted this threat speaks volumes for the metamorphosis which this once daredevil rake-hell must have undergone.

Hill's paranoia grew. He announced himself 'President of the Commonwealth'

Above: Portrait of Joshua Hill – George Eliot. The picture is captioned: 'Hill. The self-constituted King of Pitcairn's – An Impostor'.

and introduced a law which would punish those guilty of 'high treason'. John Evans had the nerve to ask if he might be able to see a copy of this proclamation, at which Hill pronounced him guilty of contempt and sentenced him to a dozen lashes. (It is not known whether he brought the cat-o'-nine-tails with him or had it specially made.)

For the 'crime' of fathering two illegitimate children *before* Hill's arrival, Buffett was tied to the church entrance and given three dozen lashes.

Within a few months, the impostor had driven Nobbs, Buffett and Evans into exile, Nobbs to Tahiti and the other two to the Gambier Islands. He now decided it was time to inform the British aristocracy of his importance. In an amazing 'memorandum' written to Lord James Townshend, he presented his credentials:

I have lived a considerable while in a palace, and had my dinner parties w1ith a princess on my right, and a General's lady upon my left.

I have drove a curricle with two outriders . . . a valet, coachman, footman, groom and, upon extraordinary occasions, my maître d'hôtel.

I have given the arm to Lady Hamilton . . . I have entertained Governors, Generals, Captains (R.N.) on board my ship . . . I have visited the Falls of Niagara and Montmorency, the natural bridge in Virginia, the great Reciprocating Fountain in East Tennessee, the great Temple of Elephanta at Bombay . . . I have visited and conversed with 'Red Jacket', the great Indian warrior . . . I have visited and been visited by a bishop . . . I have frequently partook of the delicious Hungarian wine (tokay) . . . *and Prince Swartzerburgh's old hock, said to have been 73 years old . . . I have dined with a principal Hong Kong merchant at Canton . . . I was at Napoleon's coronation . . . I have had a beautiful Egyptian Lady write to me . . .*

He informed His Lordship that he had rendered sterling service to the missionaries at the Sandwich Islands and Tahiti and reproved them for not acting on his suggestion to form a Temperance Society, then went on to explain how his precepts had led to a wondrous purification of the Pitcairners, particularly since he had removed the evil influence of Nobbs, Buffett and Evans. As justification for this action, he included a 'Humble Petition', purporting to have come from 'the Principal Native Inhabitants of Pitcairn's Island'.

The writing style makes it apparent that the 'Petition' was written by Hill himself, perhaps with the sanction of a couple of sycophants.

We, the undersigned public functionaries of Pitcairn's Island, humbly beg leave to address your Lordship, and thus implore, that your Lordship will be pleased to have pity on us, and take cognizance of our truly unfortunate case.

Your Lordship will, in the first place, be pleased to understand, that ever since the death of old Mr. John Adams (i.e. Alexander Smith of H.B.M.S. Bounty), now about five years, we have been divided in party spirit, through the presence alone of three worthless fellows (runaway English sailors, whom, alas! we allowed to stop on the island), by the names of John Buffett, George Nobbs, and John Evans.

At times we have had two schools and two churches, whilst at other times we had neither one nor the other, and at best very deficient, as may naturally be supposed; until the month of October, 1832, when Mr. Joshua Hill, an English gentleman (our actual teacher and pastor), providently, as we conceive, arrived here on the barque Pomare from Tahiti, where, it would seem, he had been doing them all the good in his power...

The bland acceptance of this epistle convinced Hill of his total ability to have his actions sanctioned, not only by the simple locals but by the highest peers of the British realm. Thus, when the 12-year-old Charlotte Quintal was found guilty of stealing some yams, he proclaimed that she would be executed! When her father objected, Hill produced a sword, put it to Quintal's throat and cried: 'Confess your sins or you are a dead man!' The old man grasped the sword with his bare hands, allowing several bystanders to disarm Hill and confiscate the sword.

The execution order was rescinded.

Convinced at last that Hill was mad, several of the islanders now wrote to George Hunn Nobbs, pleading for his return. Nobbs arrived back on 13th October, 1834, accompanied by Evans and his family, and despite Hill's violent protests, remained.

When H.M.S. *Actaeon* visited in 1837, Hill finally overreached himself. He informed the captain that he was 'a very near relative of the Duke of Bedford' and that 'the Duchess seldom rode out in her carriage without him'. He was somewhat taken aback to be informed that the captain, Lord Edward Russell, was the said Duke's eldest son, and that he had never heard of Hill. At last unmasked, the 'President of the Commonwealth of Pitcairn' was shortly thereafter removed to Valparaiso. Undaunted,

he made his way to England where he wrote a 'memorandum' to the Government, demanding payment for his six years of service to Pitcairn!

The community was united under Magistrate Edward Quintal and a set of ten laws was drawn up.†

Unique in history, the Pitcairn Laws offer an insight into the islanders' priorities and their virtually unprecedented dedication to conservation, education and democracy.

They were the first people in the world to give women the vote (1838)‡ – a distinction wrongly laid claim to by Australia (1894 in South Australia and not until 1908 in Victoria). They were also probably the first to make education compulsory. With no one like Hill to fulminate against Evil, it apparently ceased to exist, as crimes such as robbery, rape and murder do not rate a mention.

Tranquility had returned at last to the Rock of the West. And 3,700 miles away, a whisper of hope ran through the penal settlement on Norfolk Island . . .

† *See Appendix 2.*
‡ *When Sir William Dennison visited Norfolk Island in 1857 to reframe the Pitcairn Laws he agreed to leave unchanged the law which allowed women a vote in the annual election of the Chief Magistrate, but commented: 'I should most certainly not have proposed even this small amount of petticoat government had I not found it already in existence'.*

Next spread: Nobbs's 1847 letter describing Hill's régime

HELL AND PARADISE

Honourable Sir,

On the twenty-sixth of February last H.B.S. Spy arrived here bringing your very acceptable present and most interesting letters. At a meeting held shortly after, at which all the inhabitants over eighteen Years of age (male and female) were present I was requested to write a letter of thanks in the name and on behalf of the whole community, and I now take up my pen for that purpose. — From the tenor of Your letters, and the unqualified regard You are pleased to express for the welfare, spiritual and temporal, of our little commonwealth, I am sure You will be pleased to learn, that the report which reached Your ear of the "Splitting into parties" &c. is entirely without foundation. — Several Years since a partially deranged impostor, as much an object of pity as disgust, arrived here from Tahiti, as "Ambassador from England, to adjust the internal affairs of the Islands in these. He asserted that all the British ships of war on this side Cape Horn were under his immediate control, and that whoever resisted his authority would be guilty of treason, and punished accordingly. Into such a ferment were these simple minded people thrown by his wicked machinations, that quarreling & fighting became the order of the day, and that murder was not actually committed, can only be attributed to the merciful interposition of Divine providence. At length a memorial was transmitted to the British Government and Admiral Ross caused Hill to be removed from the island. — Previous to the arrival of this wicked and infatuated man, Brotherly love and kindness obtained in trust Honourable Sir you will not be offended at the familiarity I have used in this very desultory epistle, but I have been emboldened to do so from the whole tenor of your letters; which are so imbued with the milk of human kindness, — And do express so much anxiety for the welfare of the people under my care. —

I will trouble you with a letter occasionally, if I have permission and can obtain your address.

George H Nobbs Pastor

Charles Christian Magistrate
Simon Young Councillor
John Adams — Councillor

Capt. Charles Hope R. N.

CHAPTER 15

Reform and Reaction on Norfolk

In 1837, a seemingly quiet and circumspect man called Alexander Maconochie went to Hobart Town as Private Secretary to the Governor. He had made a study of prison methods in Van Diemen's Land and formulated a theory of moral reform based on incentive. It was an idea far ahead of its time but Maconochie's vigorous pamphleteering was persuasive. He reported that in New South Wales two million lashes had been administered in a seven year period. At Port Arthur, one in every four convicts was flogged; in the school, one in two boys was caned, the average number of strokes being twenty. 'The Convict System is cruel, uncertain and prodigal', he wrote. 'Instead of reforming, it degrades humanity, vitiates all under its influence . . . retards improvement and is, in many instances . . . the direct occasion of vice and crime'. He proposed a system based on 'progressive degrees of freedom according to conduct, and the abuse of them checked by motives drawn from self-interest'.

In 1840 he was appointed Commandant of Norfolk Island, amidst a great outcry from those who considered Maconochie's theories to be blind idealism. In a letter to Sir George Back, Maconochie's wife wrote:

Alexander is like a lion at bay, deafened by the barking and yelping of the curs about him but in no way stirred from his steady honesty of purpose.

Maconochie wrote:

The Cause has now got me completely . . . I will go the 'whole hog' on it . . . I have hitherto been known for a quiet and judicious person enough; and if I now appear extravagant do not at once pronounce that I have sniffed Gas . . . but examine the case – read, mark, learn and become excited yourself.

He arrived in Norfolk on the 6th of March and was appalled by what greeted him.

'The most formidable sight I ever beheld', he wrote, 'was the sea of faces upheld to me when I walked ashore . . . I found the island a turbulent, brutal Hell'.

Maconochie determined to change this and to a very large degree he succeeded. He introduced a system based on marks: so many for good behaviour, so many for good work, so

Far left: Alexander Maconochie – from the book by J. V. Barry
Left: Manacles
Below: 'The Landing Place, Norfolk Island', 1846 – pencil sketch signed A. M.

Above: Kingstown in 1848
Below: Playbill of an entertainment produced by the convicts with Maconochie's encouragement – Public Record Office, London
Above right: Martin Cash, bushranger – sketch by Thomas Bock
Right: Two aspects of the plaster death mask of 'Jacky-Jacky'

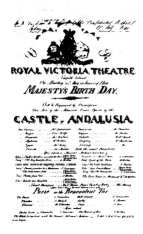

many deducted for laziness, bad language and so on. He encouraged the prisoners to play musical instruments, to form choirs and to stage their own dramas and comic operas. And he virtually abolished the gallows and the cat-o'-nine-tails.

On Queen Victoria's birthday he announced, to the horror of his civil staff, that the convicts would be included in the celebrations. A 21-gun salute was fired, the cell doors were thrown open and the men set free to wander the island, to paddle in the sea or lie in the sun unfettered. Maconochie sat down and ate with them and served a concoction of rum and Norfolk lemon as a Loyal Toast. When he called for 'Three cheers for our young queen!', the men cheered themselves hoarse.

An entertainment followed: a comic opera, a snatch of Shakespeare, ballads, glees and dances, all performed by convicts against scenery and to music created by convicts.

Maconochie was much heartened to be able to report that not one incidence of misdemeanour occurred and that the men could at last envisage the rewards of good behaviour.

The spirit and health of the men gradually improved as they began to realise that it was possible to avoid punishment if they played their part. Under a less humane rule than Maconochie's, the amazing Thomas Saulsbury Wright would not have survived a month. Arriving on Norfolk in chains at the amazing age of 102, he survived a further three years.

Known as 'Tommy the Banker', Wright was convicted of forgery in 1839 at the age of 101. Court records, and also the 1828 census, attest to this fact. Charged with having in his possession eight thousand pounds' worth of counterfeit Australian banknotes, Tommy claimed he had 'as much right as any man to start a bank'. When he finally went to the big bank in the sky, it appears that he truly was 105 years of age.

So well did Maconochie's system work that by 1843, 509 of the 593 New Hands had earned their tickets of leave. But Maconochie was a shining example of how humanity and incentive can create hope and how, all too often, religious dogma can destroy it. Bishop Ullathorne gave staunch support to him but he was undermined by a zealous priest named McEnroe who spent several years on Norfolk during Maconochie's rule. McEnroe's major contribution to the convicts' welfare was to build for them a 'neat chapel under the invocation of St. Vincent de Paul, the apostle of the galley slaves of France', and to write an extremely prolix book exposing the 'heresies' which had eroded the True Faith, from the Gnostics through Martin Luther to John Knox and Cornelius Jansen.

McEnroe returned to England, became an archdeacon, and, from this eminence, informed certain authorities that Maconochie, whilst an admirable man, was too 'soft' for the job. In 1842, he wrote to Governor Gipps:

He expects to make good subjects out of bad ones, by good feeding, good clothing, some amusement and light labour and by holding out a speedy prospect of returning to society to earn an honest livelihood. This is very plausible and very fine in theory, but he does not seem to pay proper attention to the constituent parts of the dregs of human nature on which he is experimenting.

Thus, the most enlightened prison reformist in the world was dismissed from his Norfolk post and replaced with the disciplinarian, Major Childs.

The new Commandant immediately issued new regulations. Convicts must work ceaselessly for the Government, never for themselves. No remissions were to be earned for good behaviour or good work, no private gardens were to be planted. The lash was to be used with unremitting vigour. The officers had a quaint expression for their attendance at a flogging: they called it 'going to the races'.

In 1846, as a New Year's gesture to the prisoners, Major Childs promulgated one of his more mindless and callous regulations, removing the convicts' right to grow their own vegetables. In June, this was followed by an even more senseless and provocative act. He confiscated the last of the pitiably few pleasures left in their lives, the utensils in which they roasted a portion of their ration of maize meal to mix with warm water and form a rough substitute for coffee.

An infuriated mob, led by the infamous

'Jacky-Jacky' Westwood, stormed the cookhouse. Martin Cash, reformed bushranger, was an eye-witness to these events.

'With one blow from a club', he wrote, Jacky-Jacky killed an overseer, then, encountering a watchman who was crouching, paralysed with fear, he 'spattered his brains'. Discarding the club in favour of an axe, he 'entered a hut and clove the skull of a constable'. When another constable endeavoured to reason with him, he 'struck him down and literally cut him to pieces'.

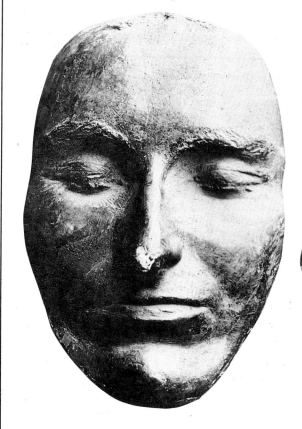

R.VHODGE LITH.

Stipendiary Magistrate Barrow wrote that he rushed to the lumberyard where he encountered 'the murdered, horribly mangled mutilated corpse of the unhappy victim Smith'.

. . . a cry reached me that two more men were nearly murdered and dying at the Lime Kiln police hut . . . I speedily hastened there and one of the most frightful bloody spectacles met my sight . . . on one stretcher opposite me lay a sub-constable named Saxton, with his forehead completely laid open so that I could see into the cavity of the head. Another frightful gash, from the eye down to the cheek, gaped so fearfully as to render the roof of the mouth quite perceptible . . . and another horrible wound in the back of the head . . . My attention was arrested by the groan of another man . . . I went into the room and a more terrifying sickening sight I never witnessed; there lay the almost lifeless body of this unhappy victim, with one side of his face completely smashed in . . . To attribute the recent painful exhibitions of a thirst for blood to the mere depriving of an unsanctioned indulgence, is, in my opinion, a perfect fallacy.

Though Westwood alone had committed all the slaughter, he was joined on the gallows by 11 others, including Kavenagh, one of Martin Cash's original gang. Their remains lie just outside the cemetery under a grassy knoll called to this day 'Murderer's Mound'.†

Cash commented in his autobiography that Westwood was simply 'tired of life . . . He had been flogged, goaded and tantalised, till he was reduced to a lunatic and a savage'.

Westwood was one of those extraordinary spirits whose sheer indomitability is incomprehensible to a twentieth century mind. A highwayman at 16, he was transported to

Australia where he escaped, returned to 'the craft of bushranging' and adopted as a defiant nickname the name of an aboriginal whom he believed had been unjustly hanged.

Following many adventures, he was captured, escaped, recaptured and escaped over and over again. This pattern continued throughout his life, in Botany Bay, Hobart Town and Norfolk Island. Liberty was so sweet to Jacky-Jacky that he would willingly snatch a few hours of it in full knowledge of the ghastly retribution which would inexorably follow.

In this mould was another of Major Childs's charges, Dennis Doherty. Sentenced at Guernsey, in the Channel Islands, for desertion from the 16th Lancers when he was a mere boy, Doherty, in the words of Anthony Trollope, spent:

*... a whole life of torment ... **forty two years of it** ... always escaping, always rebelling, always fighting against authority, and always being flogged ... Yet he talked so gently and so well, and argued his own case with such winning words! He was writing a book when we entered his cell, and was engaged on some speculation as to the tonnage of vessels. 'Just scribbling, sir,' he said, 'to while away the hours.'*

For those of a mind to peruse documentation of how much the human spirit can survive, Doherty's conduct record is preserved in the Tasmanian convict archives.

Bishop Willson, a man of undoubted goodwill, urged the dismissal of Childs but still cried for 'strong discipline'. The authorities interpreted this plea in their own fashion and, in 1846, Childs was replaced by Commandant John Price.

† *There has been talk in the Norfolk Island Assembly of moving the cemetery fence to include the mound but, to date, nothing has been done.*

CHAPTER 16

For the Term of His Natural Life

John Price was the man upon whom Marcus Clarke modelled his character Commandant Frere in *For the Term of His Natural Life*. He did not exaggerate. The monocle that Price affected became a symbol to the convicts of all that was privileged, amoral and ruthlessly contemptuous of human suffering. Even his family crest was exquisitely appropriate: *a dragon's head in whose mouth is a human hand, dripping blood.*

His father, Sir Rose Price of Trengwainton, Cornwall, inherited great slave plantations in Jamaica but somehow managed to lose his fortune, not, however, before affording Price an education at a public school. Very little is known of his early life but somewhere he acquired an uncanny familiarity with criminal jargon and an insight into the workings of the criminal mind. The convicts were sure he must have 'done time'.

J.V. Barry wrote that Price had a 'pyschopathological love/hate relationship' with the prisoners. Price regarded them as 'less than human, with no claim to justice in a civilized sense, but his vanity nevertheless demanded that they should move in submissive terror of him'. A warped strain in his nature made it necessary for him to have their reluctant regard and grudging respect as a 'fly' man.

Price certainly had a job on his hands. In Marcus Clarke's classic, the Reverend North talks of a hard core of hardened miscreants who were:

> . . . *the refuse of Port Arthur and Cockatoo Island . . . men who are known to have murdered their companions and who boast of it. With these, the English farm labourer, the . . . ignorant mechanic, the victim of perjury or mistake, are indiscriminately herded. With these are mixed Chinamen from Hong Kong, the aborigines of New Holland, West Indian Blacks, Greeks, Caffres, and Malays, soldiers for desertion, idiots, madmen, pig-stealers and pickpockets. The dreadful place seems set apart for all that is hideous and vile in our common nature. In its recklessness, its insubordination, its filth, its despair, it realises to my mind the popular notion of Hell.*

Yet, from the summit of Mount Pitt, the same chaplain describes the scene below him as 'a summer isle of Eden, lying in dark purple sphere of sea'. In its darkest days, Norfolk still retained its power to enchant.

Far left: Portrait of John Price
Above left: The Price family crest – 'Fairbairn's Crests'
Below: The Settlement in 1852 – E. Burgess

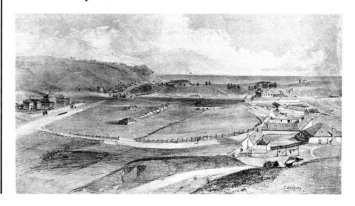

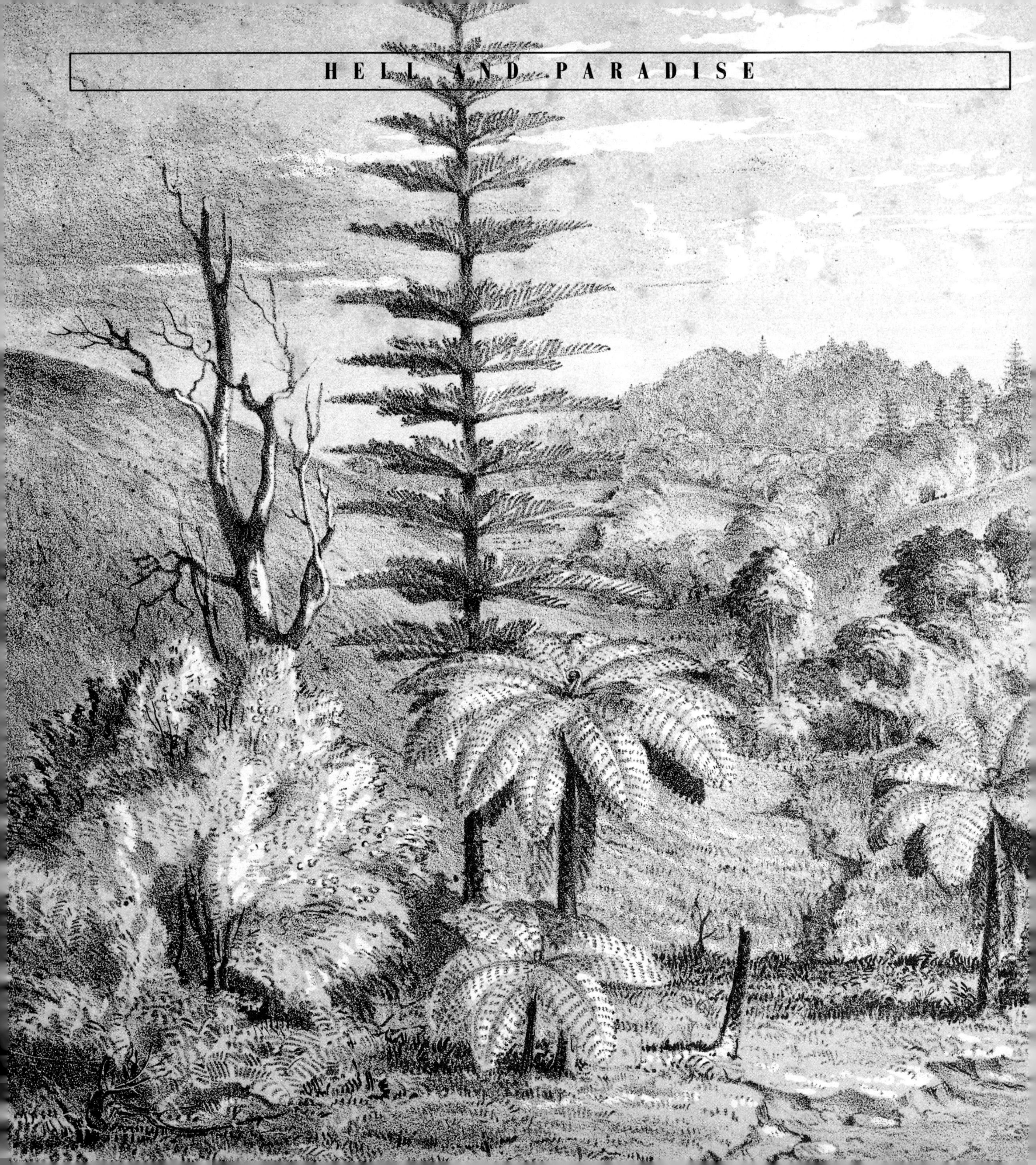

*Previous spread: 'Scene in the interior', one year before Price's arrival – J. Glen Wilson
Below: 'Seated man in stocks' – Lieut. G. F. Dashwood*

In this 'isle of Eden', the official registers record the crimes for which convicts were savagely punished:

> *For having a pipe*
> *For having fat in his possession*
> *For not walking fast enough*
> *For doing up his shoelaces when muster called*
> *For not pushing hard enough on cartload of stone*
> *.For having tobacco – later gagged for complaining*
> *For asking the Gaoler for a chew of tobacco*
> *For having a tamed bird*
> *For saying 'O my God' while on the chain*
> *For smiling while on the chain*
> *For having some ravelling from an old pair of trousers in his possession*
> *For walking across prison yard to make an enquiry*
> *For singing a song*

These offences brought penalties that were rarely less than fifty lashes or ten days imprisonment, sometimes in a cell with up to 13 others, each with standing room only.

Clarke's research was painstaking and my grandfather told me that the story of Rufus Dawes's persecution was definitely based on that of a prisoner under Price's rule.

In *For the Term of His Natural Life*, a warder picks a flower from the Commandant's garden. Rufus Dawes asks him for it, offering two days' rations in exchange. The warder gives him the sprig and Dawes takes it with tears in his eyes.

Several days later a gang are building a reef in the sea, working up to the armpits in water. They set upon the warder and beat his brains out with their shovels. The Chaplain asks Dawes why he did not intervene. 'I did all I could' is his answer. 'What's a life more or less *here!*'

Chief Warder Troke sets out to 'get' the prisoners by catching them with tobacco. They are searched going to work, at meals, going to prayers, leaving prayers, in the middle of the night. Foiled, he 'plants' a fig of tobacco, attaching a line to it and hiding in the bushes until some unfortunate convict should take the bait. Unsuccessful still, he decides to incriminate Dawes through his friendship with Blind Mooney.

Warder Troke crept close to the sleeping Dawes and, counterfeiting Mooney's mumbling utterance, asked for 'some tobacco'. Rufus Dawes was but half awake, and on repeating the request, Troke felt something put into his hand. He grasped Dawes's arm and struck a light. He had got his man this time. Dawes had conveyed to his fancied friend a piece of tobacco almost as big as the top joint of his little finger.

Dawes no sooner saw the hated face of Warder Troke peering over his hammock than he sprang out and exerting to the utmost his powerful muscles, knocked Mr. Troke fairly off his legs into the arms of the in-coming constables. A desperate struggle took place, at the end of which, the convict, overpowered by numbers, was born senseless to the cells, gagged, and chained to a ring-bolt on the bare flags. While in this condition he was savagely beaten by five or six constables.

The tortures recounted in *For the Term of His Natural Life* are authenticated in contemporary reports. Like Dawes, many prisoners spent months in solitary confinement, interrupted only by floggings, and periods up to four days' grinding cayenne pepper.

When Dawes, emaciated, blistered, blinded, broke down and cried, 'For God's sake, Captain . . . kill me at once!', he received the reply 'No fear'. That is precisely the response that Price was often known to make.

Dr. Graham, a surgeon on the island even before Price's time, describes 'the scavenger's daughter', a method of trussing a man into a kind of living parcel for up to three days, crippling him for life.

'But all are less', wrote Graham, 'than the torture of the bridle gag'. This was a perfectly-made bridle with a head-band, a throat-lash and a bit made from a four-inch ironwood tube which completely stuffed the man's mouth. A small hole in the tube allowed him to just barely breathe, his frantic attempts to do so coming out in a low whistle.

There was a tale told in my family that Clarke's character, Blind Mooney, was based on Charles McLennan†, who was convicted when he was 14 years old, and somehow sustained life through terms in the First and Second Settlements and in Van Diemen's Land. Unfortunately, I can find no evidence to corroborate this.

But Clarke's deeply moving story of Mooney's death by ballot (in which a group of prisoners draw straws to decide which one of them is to be mercifully killed by the others) is based on a ritual which is documented in a 'Report of a Select Committee, 1838':

Two or three men murdered their fellow prisoners, with the certainty of being detected and executed, apparently without malice and with very little excitement, stating that they knew they should be hanged, but it was better than being where they were.

At last the clergy were stirred to action.

Throughout these final, ghastly years, men like Bishop Ullathorne and Bishop Willson protested strenuously to the British Government and slowly their voices were heard. In 1854, the colony was totally abandoned and its convicts transported to Port Arthur in Van Diemen's Land, some of them finishing their days in the town named New Norfolk.

Commandant Price was appointed Inspector General of Convicts in Victoria where at last he received his desserts. He fixed his arrogant, monocled stare upon a group of convicts once too often and was beaten, kicked and gouged to death.

For the second time in her history, Norfolk Island was purged of evil. Eden awaited a race that would not blaspheme her.

† *See Chapter 1.*

Below: Scene with cows, 1852 – C. S. Akers

CHAPTER 17

Pitcairn to Norfolk

A dozen years of relative tranquility followed the departure from Pitcairn of the odious Joshua Hill. When Captain Wood of H.M.S. *Pandora*† visited the island, sixty years after the burning of the *Bounty*, he found the community in fine shape.

The Captain reported:

The children are not swaddled and tormented as they are in England, in consequence of which they are strong and independent looking, not an ill-formed or deformed child was to be seen; they go into the water when very young, which tans their skins and renders them some shades darker than their original colour. The women are as expert as the men in the surf, some of them being able to swim entirely round the island.

The way they effect a landing is thus: One whose experience can be trusted mounts a rock that commands a view of the sea, watches for the proper moment, when, at a signal from him, the boat which has been lying as close to the breakers as possible makes a rush and, by taking one of the less heavy breakers, goes flying in before it, frequently without a stroke of the oars being necessary except to steer her. . . a trifling deviation on either side would dash it to pieces on the rocks.

I soon found my cap ornamented with a garland of flowers and, amidst laughter and jokes, we began to ascend the cliffs. This is no easy task, even to a strong man, and to me would have been quite impracticable had not Mr. Nobbs called to one of the ladies to help me – two or three volunteered, but my prop and support was Jemima Young, a stout, good natured girl, who seized my arm and almost carried me up without the aid of my feet.

At the top of the Hill of Difficulty, as the ascent was known, 'the entire sisterhood crowded around me, and, as I could not shake all their hands at once, I thought it better to kiss them, and they appeared to like this as well'.

George Hunn Nobbs impressed all of the visitors and, by dint of tireless correspondence, recruited a band of well-to-do British patrons.

In 1852, the Pitcairners informed a visiting Rear-Admiral that they had a great desire to have their Pastor ordained. The Admiral arranged to provide Nobbs with a passage to London via Valparaiso, to give him £100 pocket money and to provide clothing appropriate in relation to the important people he would be meeting.

It was a triumphal tour. Nobbs was duly ordained in the Parish Church of Saint Mary's, Islington, given an audience with the Queen and presented with portraits of Her Majesty, Prince Albert and the royal children to be taken back to her loyal subjects in Pitcairn. The Society for the Propagation of the Gospel granted the Pastor an annual salary of £50; other generous friends donated a whale-boat, a bell for the church, tools, medicine, clothing, furniture and

Far left: Ann Naomi and Jane Nobbs, taken one year after the Pitcairners landed in Norfolk
Above left: 'Pacific Parrakeet'
Above: George Hunn Nobbs, after his inordination

† *Coincidentally the namesake of the vessel which unsuccessfully sought the last of the mutineers in 1790.*

£500 for the future benefit of the flock.

However, the Pitcairners were soon finding their tiny island increasingly unable to support them. Of its one and three quarter square miles, only 8% (88 acres) is flat land and there were now close to 200 mouths to feed. Compounding the problem was the scarcity of fish; they had deserted the coastal waters following a storm in 1845 which caused massive landslides.

In 1855, the elders wrote to Queen Victoria, humbly begging for help. In one of the most generous gestures in the Empire's history, she offered them Norfolk Island.

Thirty-four persons at first declined the offer, but finally, on the 3rd of May, 1856, the entire Pitcairn community sailed for Norfolk on the *Morayshire*.

That community comprised a total of 193 souls but just eight family names covered them all: Christian, Quintal, Adams, McCoy and Young, descendants of the mutineers; and Buffett, Evans and Nobbs, the progeny of the only other three persons to be allowed to settle on Pitcairn. Yet there was not a trace of an in-breeding problem.†

After a miserable five-week trip, during which virtually the entire ship's complement was hideously seasick for the entire 3,700 miles and during which a baby was born, the *Morayshire* arrived at Norfolk Island on the 8th of June, 1856. The day of their landing was the anniversary of the day that the *Bounty* was commissioned.

They brought with them their Laws and Regulations – and their faith. Generous provisions awaited them. Captain Denham wrote:

Pending harvest time, I leave their community of 194 persons provided with 45,500 lbs of biscuits, flour, maize, rice, with groceries of proportion, and an abundance of milk at hand, 22 horses, 10 swine in sties, domestic fowls, 16000 lbs of hay, 5000 lbs of straw, and a number of wild pigs and fowls. And lest the first crop should fall short I have arranged with the Governor for a supply of potatoes, rice and peas as an extent of aid.

Everything about their new home astonished the Pitcairners: the massive stone buildings were veritable castles, the cattle and horses were the first they had ever seen, as were gardens of English flowers, and exotic new fruits and vegetables. The lavatories were a mystery until their use was explained.

Anything with wheels provided a novel sport – it was pushed down the nearest hill and smashed. Furniture which exceeded the bounds of pure functionality became fuel. The mopokes and the 'Ghost Birds' terrified the newcomers as did reminders of convict punishments. A gibbet which stood in front of the prison was hurled into the sea.

By now, the ex-pirate George Hunn Nobbs had been genuinely transformed and the Bishop of London would have been proud of the man he had ordained as a deacon and priest. To this new community he was was a rock; to outsiders he wrote:

Think of us, in the Church, which had formerly been occupied by the vilest outcasts of society; and then imagine us in the grave-yard filled with mounds that contained hundreds of their bodies, and you will enter largely into the feeling of gratitude, joy, grief, and I had almost said, terror, that pervaded our minds.

The Pitcairners eventually settled down to the task of consolidating their position. They learned new trades: milking, sheep-shearing,

Above: George Adams, son of John Adams

corn-grinding and ploughing. They converted the Commandant's Building to a church and restored and settled into the superb, convict-built Georgian homes on Quality Row. Understandably, they razed the interior of the hated pentagonal prison and used the stones for building. Fletcher Christian Nobbs converted the prison at Longridge into the graceful building known today as Branka House.

Bishop Selwyn, who had designated Norfolk 'the Ocean Hell' when he visited it in convict days, now wrote: 'I doubt not, that eventually the presence of the Pitcairn people will render it what nature intended it to be – an earthly paradise'.

But when Governor Sir William Dennison sent instructions for their behaviour, insisting that they were beholden to New South Wales, they were dismayed. The islanders maintained that an absolute condition of their leaving Pitcairn was that Norfolk should be ceded to them totally.

Just 18 months after their arrival, 17 members of the Young family sailed the 3700 miles back to Pitcairn. This was the first separation in a community which had been living as one family for sixty years and the parting was a fearful wrench. Albert Gazzard described the scene: '. . . one last mingling of their voices in song, pathetically and falteringly rendered, sobs choking their utterance and tears dimming their sight'.

Five years later, a second party returned to Pitcairn. It comprised Thursday October Christian's family of 12, Simon Young's family of 11, two Buffetts, and another Christian and her husband.

It was yet another horrendous journey, plagued with storm, seasickness and death. In her journal written on board the *St. Kilda*, John Buffett's sister, Mary Young, wrote on 20th January, 1864:

The wind is the same, just after breakfast Thursday's little girl died. They put her in salt to preserve the body that she may be buried on shore.

The 44 returnees formed the nucleus of the third Pitcairn Island community which grew to more than 200 but which is now sadly shrunken to close to its original number.

Next spread: Pitcairners after the return to their island

† *Because of their close intermarriage over many generations, the Pitcairners were ideal subjects for anthropological study and this led Harry L. Shapiro, later president of the American Anthropological Association, to make his home on Pitcairn and produce three books which became the definitive works on line-breeding. Not a vestige of genetic deterioration was found and it is now accepted that, provided the initial gene pool is without flaw, this form of breeding is as sound as any other. In fact, it is now known that the crossing of dissimilar genetic lines produces a phenomenon known as 'hybrid vigour'. For several generations the Pitcairners' enforced choice of cousin-spouses actually improved the stock.*

Above: The 'Morayshire' – photograph bequeathed to the Mitchell Library, Sydney, by Captain L. C. Boulton

CHAPTER 18

'God's Gentlemen' and Others

In 1866, the Melanesian Mission, after much lobbying in Britain and New South Wales, set up its headquarters on Norfolk. This was an organisation involved in the recruiting and evangelising of natives from scores of islands around the Pacific. George Hunn Nobbs resented what he saw as a land-grab and indulged in a little overkill in a harangue opposing 'so very undesirable an addition to our social circle as a hundred or two of heathens strong with the odour of unmitigated depravity'. In fact, the Mission posed no spiritual threat to the Pitcairners – it was the rest of the Pacific it was destined to pollute.

Victorian England had an overweening zeal for Christianising the 'savages' and despite the undoubted good intentions of many of the missionaries, it is difficult to find, in the whole history of the Pacific, a single instance of good following their intervention. History has repeatedly demonstrated that the natives were essentially attracted to Christianity out of a belief that it could bring them material goods; then, as even now in parts of the Pacific, it was a kind of cargo cult. Many of the evangelists were well aware of this: the indefatigable John Williams, who became a super-hero of the London Missionary Society, wrote with relish of the thinking processes of the Samoan chiefs:

Can the religion of these wonderful papalangis† be anything but wise and good? . . . their heads are covered, while ours are exposed to the heat of the sun and the wet of the rain, their bodies are clothed all over with beautiful cloth, while we have nothing but a bandage of leaves around our waist; they have clothes upon their very feet, while ours are like the dogs' – and then look at their axes, their scissors, and their other property – how rich they are!

Missions paved the way for commerce, Williams proclaimed. Once the natives had undergone this civilising process, 'think of hundreds and thousands of them wearing European clothing and using European articles, such as tools . . .'.

† *White men*

Far left and below: The Melanesian Mission
Left: House, Norfolk Island

A few decades later, Paul Gauguin was to see the missionaries as 'plunderers of native culture', reducing their own and the natives' lives to a 'stupefying dullness'. Robert Louis Stevenson called their activities 'practically soul-murder'.

Twenty years before the Melanesian Mission came to Norfolk, Herman Melville, author of *Moby Dick*, issued a warning to the zealous do-gooders of America and England: he maintained that it would have made more sense had the natives of the Pacific reversed roles and gone as missionaries to the 'civilized' countries to teach them South Sea philosophies. But his was a rare voice.

Bishop Selwyn, of New Zealand's Church of England, was fired with a passion to extend his crusading activities to all of Polynesia and Melanesia, and was delighted when fate, or diligence, turned up an error in the letters patent which described the boundaries of his diocese. Discovering that his northern boundary was given as 34° 30′ north, rather than south, he seized the opportunity.

It must be said to Governor Dennison's credit that when Selwyn attempted to persuade him to grant Pitcairner land for a Mission, he refused. Nothing daunted, Selwyn then proposed that the island be ruled by a triumvirate comprising one person chosen by the Governor, one by the Pitcairners and . . . himself. He was unsuccessful in this modest request but, following further overtures to the new Governor, Sir John Young, by the first Bishop of Melanesia, John Coleridge Patteson, permission was granted for the Mission to purchase 933 acres at $4 per acre. A further 99 acres was handed to them, free.

By the time the magnificent 'Bishopscourt' was built as a home for Patteson, 190 boys and girls from 30 different islands were being indoctrinated on Norfolk, preparatory to being shipped back to their home islands, there to continue the cycle of evangelisation.

In 1871, John Patteson went on a recruiting mission to the Solomon Islands, where he was killed by the natives. The extraordinary St. Barnabas Chapel was built in his memory.

Of all the buildings one would not expect to find on a Pacific island, this surely must be it. Designed in England, with stained glass windows by the illustrious Burne-Jones, it was interpreted and brought into existence by the unlikely partnership of Melanesian mission boys and Norfolk craftsmen. To provide building stones, the latter tore down sections of the hated Kingston prison. The result is a building with an extraordinary ambience – a blend of South Sea and British architecture and decoration that is unique.

But many of the Pitcairners were not impressed, even with this gentle and graceful monument. Anything to do with the Mission was a burr in their minds because they still considered it had trespassed on their domain (thus beginning the process they feared would gradually dispossess them). They claimed, as had their forebears, and as did their descendants for more than a century, that Her Majesty Queen Victoria had ceded the entire island to them. They insisted that there was an actual 'Paper of Cession' which had been handed to their magistrate, Frederick Young. Thus, when one-ninth of the island was occupied by the Mission, they felt betrayed.

But the document – the keystone of their rights – had mysteriously disappeared.†

Not only were their land rights lost but

their attempts at trade with the outside world were met with unremitting frustration. The list of short-lived booms and inevitable busts is formidable: lemons, kumaras, bananas, onions, whale oil, fungi, arrowroot, passion-fruit, bean seed, Tung Oil trees, pine and vegetable seeds . . .

Isolation, the cost and irregularity of shipping, disease, fashion – all played their role in thwarting Norfolk's aspirations. Of all its attempts at agriculture, only palm seed and seedlings have ever made a steady contribution to its economy.

Yet, through all these bursts of activity and disappointment, the islanders maintained a unique serenity. The words of Beatrice

† *See Appendix 3.*

Below: St. Barnabas Chapel – colour postcard, 1909

Grimshaw, written in the early 1900s, describe an appealing people:

Every Norfolker, barefoot, uneducated, and unversed in the ways of the world of society though he may be, is nevertheless a gentleman in all the essentials. The quiet self-possession, the low, pleasant voice, the easy courtesy shown by the Norfolker to any stranger, whether the latter be a globe-trotting peer, or a broken-down sailor run away from his ship, can only be matched elsewhere in what is known as 'the very best' society. There is not the first trace of a snob about him . . .

Among the women, many show traces of the beauty that was the undoing of the Bounty men, long ago. Large, dark, shining eyes are

common, with long, soft hair, pleasant features and a singularly sweet smile.

The voices of all the Islanders are remarkably low and musical. They are the voices of those whose ancestors for many generations have never known hurry or anxiety; of people dwelling in 'a land where it is always afternoon' – of a gentle, dreamy folk, living slow, sweet lives as changeless as the empty sea that rings round their island home.

The sentiment was genuine but the sea was not changeless and it was not empty. It varied from mill-pond to cauldron and it held fish and whales. The massive digester at Cascade is the sole memorial to Norfolk's whaling days. Two hundred years ago, whales were frequently seen rubbing off their barnacles on the rocks of Cascade Bay and it is recorded that the gentle giants would miraculously find a passage through the reef into Emily Bay (then Turtle Bay), where they would mate and calve.

American whalers began calling at Norfolk to reprovision during the early days of the Third Settlement. Mrs. Parnell Pease, the wife of one of the American whaling captains, describes in her diary the method by which a lady came ashore on Cascade jetty in those days: 'On the crest of a surge, I was hurled from the strongest oarsman's arms to the arms of a tall man on the pier'.

The Pitcairners, with their maritime background, soon found themselves serving on the American ships. (Fletcher Christian's great grandson was one.) Swiftly learning this arduous and dangerous trade, the islanders set up in business for themselves. Normally unenamoured of the work ethic – a legacy of their Tahitian blood, these men showed remarkable dedication and fortitude when the

sea-going side of their heritage was invoked.

A visitor to the island in the early 1900s wrote:

There are no finer boatmen, no more daring whalers, in all of the Pacific, than these indolent dreamers, when the mood for action is on them.

Previous spread: Interior of St. Barnabas Chapel
Far left: Leonard Christian of Pitcairn with Miss Nobbs of Norfolk
Below left: 'Maria Christian, Ellen Quintal and Sarah M'Koy' – 1854
Below: Whale boats – Hotchkiss gun for shooting whales

Previous spread: Cutting out the harpoon – 1922 photo
Above: Humpback with crowd – whaling station
Right: George Hunn Nobbs in the last year of his life

The harpooner, holding the crew's life in his hands, must 'make fast' with his first iron or risk having the boat crushed with a stroke of the whale's massive, flailing flukes.

Then would follow an all-day and frequently all-night towing, with the women, and often the children, standing on the cliffs singing hymns and praying that the whaleboat's lantern would not disappear, signifying that the whale had dragged their menfolk to an ocean grave. One of their hymns, a relic of whaling days, is still sung on the island:

Brightly beams our Father's mercy
From his lighthouse ever more
But to us he gives the keeping
Of the lights along the shore.

Let the lower lights be burning!
Send a gleam across the wave
Some poor fainting, struggling seaman
You may rescue, you may save . . .

George Hunn Nobbs continued to act as pastor until the day he died. He gradually learned to accept the Melanesian Mission but protected the interests of his own flock with undiminished devotion. His position in the community was summed up by the Reverend Elcum of the Mission in 1880:

Whenever I helped on Sunday mornings, I was always expected to join the venerable Pastor's patriarchal family circle at dinner, often numbering twenty to thirty people, three generations being represented, the younger acting as waiters to their seniors, and sitting down when they had left the table. There was something very courtly about this simple yet religious ménage. Mr. Nobbs himself seemed so thoroughly to respect himself, and to be respected, that I often thought of Abraham and other world heads of families, in whose home

The boat would be launched at dawn and would sail quietly over the grey water until a spout announced the presence of a whale, sometimes a sperm, more usually a humpback. Once the whale sounded, the skipper would have the task of predicting where it would surface. He must manoeuvre his boat close to the monster but not directly above it.

circles discipline and gravity were always kept up, though never felt to be irksome because all was done in the love and fear of God.

Nobbs died in 1884, aged 85, leaving a widow, 10 children, 65 grandchildren, and 19 great-grandchildren. There were 470 souls in the community. 470 attended the funeral.

Adventurer, pirate and opportunist until the age of 30, George Hunn Nobbs had thereafter devoted a remarkable 55 years to the spiritual and temporal leadership of Pitcairn and Norfolk Islands. He is revered to this day. The epitaph on his tombstone is singularly appropriate: 'By the Grace of God, I am what I am!'

In 1902, Norfolk became a part of Britain's 'electric girdle of the Empire' when a cable station was built at Anson Bay and the island became a link in a system which transmitted morse code dots and dashes over a route stretching from Vancouver to Australia and New Zealand.†

This encouraged more attempts to sell Norfolk's produce to the world but success was scant. Nevertheless, the life-style was one which more prosperous nations looked upon with some envy, as evidenced by the following page from a 1921 issue of the *Sydney Mail*.

In 1925, the islanders' dream of owning a trading ship was realised when they built, from local pine, an 18-metre schooner they named *Resolution*. They launched her with great ceremony in Emily Bay but her initial voyage was a disaster, taking so long that her cargo of

† *A new Pacific submarine cable, ANZCAN (Australia, New Zealand, Canada), is now in place, giving the island access to 1200 channels in place of the single channel provided by the original.*

The following is a reproduction of a newspaper clipping:

LEMON JUICE AND PEEL INDUSTRY OF NORFOLK ISLAND

A MAGNIFICENT AVENUE OF NORFOLK ISLAND PINES.
It is a mile and a half long, and was planted well over 100 years ago.

CASCADE, THE SAFEST LANDING-PLACE ON THE ISLAND.
The lack of a good harbour is the greatest drawback to trade development.

NORFOLK ISLAND, which is only 8600 acres in extent, is famous for its beautiful climate, which is anything but tropic. It has an even, cool temperature all the year round, and is accounted by many the healthiest spot on earth. It is also the fairest, richest, and most fertile of islands—"a little bit of England in the summer time." To the tourist in search of beauty; to the seeker after health and rest it is the ideal sanatorium. It is a land of perpetual verdure, of many lovely hills and valleys, the home of the tall, great-girthed, stately Norfolk pines, gigantic trees many of them, with wide-spreading branches, and discernible out at sea for many, many miles. Norfolk is also the land of plenty, where all fruits grow wild and luxuriantly, where high cost of living is impossible, and the profiteer cannot abide in his wickedness. A land of 800 inhabitants and not one politician. Industrialism can find no beginning in Norfolk, as the capitalist and labourer are one and the same person. It is a happy land of good, kind, hospitable folk, who are not black in colour, as many people seem to think.

The Norfolk islanders, as they are generally called—a name which suggests that they are a native black race—are descended from some remarkable Britons, the mutineers of the British warship Bounty. The story of their seizure of Lieutenant Bligh's ship is well known. The Norfolk folk to-day are proud of their forebears. When volunteers were leaving for France in 1914 they were addressed by one of their elders, who said, "Go, my boys; show the world the mettle that is in you; show the world you are possessed of the same blood and the same courage of men who dared to do what few have done—seize a British ship of war." And right worthily did these volunteers prove their mettle and their courage. On the fields of France they fought nobly, and died, many of them, with the pluck that is their heritage.

In these days of grace this picturesque and charming island is budding into one of some commercial importance. The energy and enterprise of the people are manifest in a fine lemon-peel and lemon-juice industry, which is assuming some pretensions, and has even now a trade with Sydney worth many thousands of pounds sterling annually. Recently there went from the island to Sydney a shipment of 1500 casks, 600 of lemon-juice, and 900 of lemon-peel, in value equal to £15,000. Lemons grow wild all over the island; in every garden and paddock are clumps of trees ever bearing fruit in wonderful abundance. The lemon is the common variety which apparently does better without cultivation. No attempt is made on Norfolk Island to tend it in any way; yet it is a fruit of full, rich juice, with a rind most suitable for peel. Little factories,

Recently 1500 casks of lemon juice and lemon peel arrived at Sydney from Norfolk Island. It was for the Christmas market, and the demand for it showed that the quality was all that could be desired. This industry, which is only in its infancy, is capable of great expansion, and the islanders look to Australia to help them develop it.—By T. J. McMAHON.

DIRECT DESCENDANTS OF THE RINGLEADERS OF THE BOUNTY MUTINY.
These ladies—Mrs. and Miss Christian—are charming and hospitable Norfolkians. Their hands are resting on tablets made of wood from the decks of the old Bounty; on these tablets the Ten Commandments were carved by one of the mutineers over 100 years ago.

family concerns, are dotted all over the island. These factories are usually roughly-constructed wooden buildings divided into a room with long rows of sorting bins, another room for cutting and squeezing frames, and another holding great vats of brine, in which are stored and soaked the peel before it is casked. During the lemon season, and that is most of the year, Norfolk is a busy place; boys and girls are out in the fields packing and loading up tip-drays, and these are to be met coming in to the factories from every quarter. The island has many roads, made during the period when Norfolk was a convict settlement. Outside the factories are great golden heaps of lemons waiting to be sorted. Inside there is the hum of much chattering and laughter from eager, busy workers cutting and squeezing the fruit, and at hand deep troughs are running high with the golden juice. On one side are women scooping out the pulp and throwing it deftly into huge tubs, to be further pressed to extract every drop of juice. On wide tables stand miniature piles of lemon-peel, ready to be washed and prepared for the brine vats. In one season millions upon millions of lemons pass through the factories; thousands upon thousands are cut and squeezed, and stacks of peel brined in a day. The workers toil eight hours a day, and with appliances quite primitive; but they are experts at their work, and cheerful withal. The basic wage business has no interest for them. Outside the factories are rows of casks, hundreds filled with juice or packed with peel. From sheds near by comes the musical clink of coopers' hammers as they stave and rim, while more silent workers seal and brand the casks.

ON steamer days, when loading is going on, Norfolk is a very busy place. The whole island is astir, people moving about on horseback or in sulkies, every road carrying long lines of drays and slides loaded with casks, hastening to that part of the coast at which the steamer is anchored, sometimes Kingston, but more often at the Cascade, a sheltered roadstead. The one great drawback to Norfolk and its trade possibilities, and one that will perhaps seriously interfere with the regular working of the industry, is the need of a safe harbour. Wind and sea rise very quickly, and loading becomes impossible. At times a steamer will waste days drifting and steaming about, waiting for the wind and sea to moderate, Norfolk Island's shores are imposing in their grandeur, but they are boulder-strewn and blocked by inaccessible cliffs. In high seas the coast is very dangerous, and ships cannot take any risks.

Hundreds of casks are strewn along the landing-place and down the short jetty. These are either hoisted into big whaleboats or dropped into the sea and spiked and tethered together, forming long rafts, which are towed out to the steamer. Norfolk Island's skilful boatmen, and, though at most times the heavy swell of the sea makes loading difficult, the whale boats plunging dangerously about the rock landing, these sailormen handle the casks without loss or accident. There is no doubt a future for this industry, and the Norfolk people look to Australians to encourage their enterprise. Already it is successful, and in time will be extensive, for while millions upon millions of lemons are used up, there are millions upon millions of lemons still going to waste.

A BIG SHIPMENT FOR SYDNEY.
The casks are either floated out to the ship or carried thither in whale boats.

LOWERING CASKS INTO A WHALE BOAT.
The islanders are skilful boatmen, and in rough weather have many exciting experiences.

---

fruit rotted. She was never able to trade profitably and, in 1949, sank ignominiously in Port Vila harbour.

In 1930 arrived the first aircraft ever to visit Norfolk Island – a Gipsy Moth piloted by Francis Chichester, later to become Sir Francis. He had at that point flown 14,000 miles of an around-the-world solo flight and had navigated to tiny Norfolk by his own system of sun-sighting, which he continued to use in his subsequent world-circumnavigations by sea. Dense cloud obscured his vision as he arrived over the place he hoped would be Norfolk. Miraculously the clouds parted and there she lay.

Chichester landed at Cascade Bay, spent the night at Government House and prepared to take off at sunrise the following morning. After many futile runs, he discovered that one of his floats had sprung a leak and was thoroughly waterlogged. Following four days of frantic repairs, and the towing overland of the Gipsy Moth from Cascade to Emily Bay, he finally took off, to the anxious cheers of the islanders.

He undertook the 561-mile transoceanic flight to Lord Howe virtually without instruments, his compass, altimeter, air speed indicator and radio transmitter all being disabled. After seven and a half hours of flying, and almost out of fuel, something suddenly 'stabbed the air like a broad primaeval dagger of grey stone'. It was Ball's Pyramid, a 552-foot rock pinnacle a few kilometres off Lord Howe. He landed safely on the island's lagoon where the islanders stared 'as if the dodo had been found'. Next morning, he found that a hurricane had turned his Gypsy Moth upside-down in a deep water-filled depression known as Sylph's Hole.

The islanders, very few of whom had set eyes on a grounded plane, set to, ordered parts to be sent by steamer from Sydney and, within nine weeks, had repaired her. Chichester took the time to treat dozens of helpers to joy-rides, broke a bottle of brandy over the plane and endeavoured to take off, to discover that, just as in Cascade Bay, his floats were waterlogged and his radio inoperative.

Taking two carrier pigeons on board, jettisoning food, spare parts and all but eight

hours of fuel, he made it to Australia in just over six.

A dozen years were to pass until the Norfolk islanders were to see another aircraft. During the 1939-45 war, an airstrip was constructed on Norfolk for defence purposes. The only practical site was along the Avenue of Pines, the pride of the island. In his *Tales of the South Pacific*, James Michener describes them: 'Like the pillars of a vast and glorious cathedral ran the pines, a stately double column stretching for two miles toward the mountain'. They were razed, as the locals stood by in agony.

On Christmas Day, 1942, a New Zealand Air Force plane was the first to land on the airstrip and soon a force greatly outnumbering the local population was in occupation. When the war ended, the Norfolk islanders found themselves in a situation they could scarcely comprehend – they were in touch with the world. Today, 400 m.p.h. medium jets fly in almost daily.

Whaling continued on and off on Norfolk right up until 1962 when the whales just stopped coming. One theory has it that they had ruthlessly been shot out in the Antarctic. But some old-timers are convinced that, having swum this route since the beginning of time, the intelligent leviathans had finally had enough of the islanders' harpoons and had deliberately shifted their course. Over the last few years, occasional sightings have again been made, but a whaling industry will never again exist here.

When, in 1962, the final outpouring of the stench of boiling blubber had cleared from the air, Norfolk returned to the serene paradise which had been her natural state for the better part of three million years.

*Far left: Feature in 'Sydney Mail',
1921
Left: The original 'Resolution',
commanded by Captain Cook –
Harry Roberts
Next spread: Account of life on
Norfolk Island during the Twenties*

THE SYDNEY MAIL, WEDNE

LEMON JUICE AND PEEL IN

Recently 1500 casks of lemon juice and lemon peel arrived at Sydney from Norfolk Island. It was for the Christmas market, and the demand for it showed that the quality was all that could be desired. This industry, which is only in its infancy, is capable of great expansion, and the islanders look to Australia to help them develop it.—By T. J. McMAHON.

NORFOLK ISLAND, which is only 8600 acres in extent, is famous for its beautiful climate, which is anything but tropic. It has an even, cool temperature all the year round, and is accounted by many the healthiest spot on earth. It is also the fairest, richest, and most fertile of islands—"a little bit of England in the summer time." To the tourist it is a dream of beauty; to the seeker after health and rest it is the ideal sanatorium. It is a land of perpetual verdure, of many lovely hills and valleys, the home of the tall, great-girthed, stately Norfolk pines, gigantic trees many of them, with wide-spreading branches, and discernible out at sea for many, many miles. Norfolk is also the land of plenty, where all fruits grow wild and luxuriantly, where high cost of living is impossible, and the profiteer cannot abide in his wickedness. A land of no rates and taxes, and but one picture show. There are 800 inhabitants and not one politician. Industrialism can find no beginning in Norfolk, as the capitalist and labourer are one and the same person. It is a happy land of good, kind, hospitable folk, who are not black in colour, as many people seem to think.

The Norfolk Islanders, as they are generally called—a name which suggests that they are a native black race —are descended from some remarkable Britons, the mutineers of the British warship Bounty. The story of their seizure of Lieutenant Bligh's ship is well known. The Norfolk folk to-day are proud of their forebears. Wh volunteers were leaving for France in 1914 they were a dressed by one of their elders, who said. "Go, my ho show the world the mettle that is in you; show the wo you are possessed of the same blood and the same cour of men who dared to do what few have done—seize British ship of war." And right worthily did these vol teers prove their mettle and their courage. On fields of France they fought nobly, and died, many them, with the pluck that is their heritage.

In these days of grace this picturesque and charm island is budding into one of some commercial importar The energy and enterprise of the people are manifest a fine lemon-peel and lemon-juice industry, which is suming some pretensions, and has even now a trade w Sydney worth many thousands of pounds sterling annua Recently there went from the island to Sydney a sh ment of 1500 casks, 600 of lemon-juice, and 900 of lem peel, in value equal to £15,000. Lemons grow wild over the island; in every garden and paddock are clum of trees ever bearing fruit in wonderful abundance. lemon is the common variety which apparently does b ter without cultivation. No attempt is made on Norf Island to tend it in any way; yet it is a fruit of full, r juice, with a rind most suitable for peel. Little factor family concerns, are dotted all over the island. Th factories are usually roughly-constructed wooden bu ings divided into a room with long rows of sorting b another room for cutting and squeezing frames, and other holding great vats of brine, in which are sto and soaked the peel before it is casked. During lemon season, and that is most of the year, Norfolk i busy place; boys and girls are out in the fields pack and loading up tip-drays, and these are to be met con in to the factories from every quarter. The island has n roads, made during the period when Norfolk was a con settlement. Outside the factories are great golden heap lemons waiting to be sorted. Inside there is the hun much chattering and laughter from eager, busy wor cutting and squeezing the fruit, and at hand deep tro are running high with the golden juice. On one side

STRY OF NORFOLK ISLAND

nen scooping out the pulp and **throwing it deftly into** e tubs, to be further pressed **to extract every drop** uice. On wide tables stand **miniature piles of lemon-** l, ready to be washed and prepared **for the brine vats.** one season millions upon **millions of lemons pass** ugh the factories; thousands upon thousands are cut

ECT DESCENDANTS OF THE RINGLEADERS OF THE BOUNTY MUTINY.

se ladies—Mrs. and Miss Christian—are charming and hospit- Norfolkians. Their hands are resting on tablets made of wood u the decks of the old Bounty; on these tablets the Ten Com- dments were carved by one of the mutineers over 100 years ago.

and squeezed, and stacks of peel brined in a day. The workers toil eight hours a day, and with appliances quite primitive: but they are experts at their work, and cheerful withal. The basic wage business has no interest for them. Outside the factories are rows of casks, hundreds filled with juice or packed with peel. From sheds near by comes the musical clink of coopers' hammers as they stave and rim, while more silent workers seal and brand the casks.

ON steamer days, when loading is going on, Norfolk is a very busy place. The whole island is astir, people moving about on horseback or in sulkies, every road carrying long lines of drays and slides loaded with casks, hastening to that part of the coast off which the steamer is anchored, sometimes Kingston, but more often at the Cascade, a sheltered roadstead. The one great drawback to Norfolk and its trade possibilities, and one that will perhaps seriously interfere with the regular working of the industry, is the need of a safe harbour. Wind and sea rise very quickly, and loading becomes impossible. At times a steamer will waste days drifting and steaming about, waiting for the wind and sea to moderate. Norfolk Island's shores are imposing in their grandeur, but they are boulder-strewn and blocked by inaccessible cliffs. In high seas the coast is very dangerous, and ships cannot take any risks.

Hundreds of casks are strewn along the landing-place and down the short jetty. These are either hoisted into big whaleboats or dropped into the sea and spiked and tethered together, forming long rafts, which are towed out to the steamer. Norfolk Islanders are skilful boatmen, and, though at most times the heavy swell of the sea makes loading difficult, the whale boats plunging dangerously about the rock landing, these sailormen handle the casks without loss or accident. There is no doubt a future for this industry, and the Norfolk people look to Australians to encourage their enterprise. Already it is successful, and in time will be extensive, for while millions upon millions of lemons are used up, there are millions upon millions of lemons still going to waste.

APPENDIX 1

Norfolk and Pitcairn Today

Standing today on Queen Elizabeth's Lookout, gazing down on the peacock's tail colours of Emily Bay and admiring the superbly preserved colonial buildings, one can scarcely comprehend that this was the setting for the most appalling depravities in the history of British colonialism.

The island subsists principally on tourism. People of all ages come to soak up history amongst its superbly restored, originally convict-constructed buildings, or to experience, on other parts of the island, the soul-soothing tranquility which one might imagine, wrongly but so easily, had been Norfolk's throughout its history.

In the beachside cemetery, one can walk among the ghosts of the hideous penal days. At Chimney Hill and Cascade and Cemetery Bays, it is not difficult to imagine one hears the voices of the convict miners as they quarry limestone and 'dripstone' – a porous rock used for filtering water.

At Kingston, one can walk through an entire nineteenth century village, scarcely changed from the days when the enforced blacksmiths, masons, bakers, shingle-splitters, cloth and cord makers, tailors and bullockies plied their trades.

The hospital still stands and the infamous crank mill (now roofless), under whose floor are buried hundreds of artifacts awaiting disinterment for the proposed museum. Close by can still be seen one of the main sawpits where the 'top dog' would lift the saw upwards and the 'underdog' would pull it down.

There is the whole of Quality Row to explore, the extraordinary cemetery, the Commissariat's Store, the Military Barracks; and perhaps best of all: there are dozens of stunning, cliff-top perches at which to picnic and enjoy the very special Norfolk sunsets.

Norfolk's permanent population now numbers 1800 and it is rapidly adapting to change. There is now a modern airport, over fifty taxfree shops (all on one site at the centre of the island, to leave the rest unspoilt) and there are facilities for dozens of sports.

The residents are determined to keep this one of the few unspoiled places left in the world. They have placed strict limitations on the number of people who can live on the island and the number of visitors who can visit at any one time.

It is certain that some of the old customs will remain on Norfolk for a long time, most certain of them all the celebration of Anniversary Day. Every year on 8th June, just

Far left: Sea-lashed Nepean Island
Above: The Crank Mill
Below left: House on Quality Row

as they have done since 1856, the islanders don traditional dress and re-enact the landing of their ancestors at Kingston. This is followed by a walk to the Cenotaph for the laying of wreaths, then to the wonderful old cemetery where the touching Pitcairn hymns are sung. A colourful and elaborate picnic is then held at Slaughter Bay, in the windless enclosure inside the massive walls of what once was the pentagonal prison.

If you know some of the locals you might be asked to join them at their tables or ground-camps, bedecked with flowers and laden with dishes particular to the island. If not, take your own rug, food and beverage. Though waves of the strangely cadenced Pitcairnese language will wash around you, you'll feel very welcome. After a while you will become aware that everyone has a nickname. There's a simple reason: a recent count listed 55 adults with the surname Christian or Christian-Bailey, 47 Buffets, 27 Evans, 24 Quintals, 22 Adams, 19 Nobbs and 16 McCoys. All go back, at least by matrilineal descent, to the mutineers.

As evening shadows lengthen, you may fancy you hear a *Bounty* roll-call; and perhaps you will imagine you see lips move, framing the word 'Aye'. . .

To visit Pitcairn is a very different proposition. Britain's last remaining colony in the Pacific (ironically not one she founded) is in danger of perishing. The island is reduced to a dangerously low 45 souls (representing a net zero population growth over 120 years); moreover, our modern world of commerce and technology does not touch upon it, and has no need of it.

As jet aircraft and computerised container ships now cross the Pacific without need for wayside stops, the Pitcairners have little outlet for their crafts, no regular supplies, and a frighteningly tenuous access to urgent medical attention. If one of the rare ships should arrive on a Sunday, the islanders' religious beliefs ban trade with it.

A group of mainly Norfolk islanders made a recent pilgrimage to Pitcairn to mark the hundredth anniversary of the death of their legendary pastor, George Hunn Nobbs. The visit was achieved by mustering a party of 30, flying via Auckland to Tahiti, chartering a Fokker F27 for a six-hour flight to the Gambier Islands and commissioning a cargo ship, *Taporo II†*, for a 72-hour Mangareva/Pitcairn round trip of 520 nautical miles.

While the ship was still hundreds of miles from Pitcairn, one of the pilgrims, Doctor John Davey, was taken off it by helicopter and rushed to the island to accompany a suspected gangrene case back to Mangareva. (Pitcairn has had no resident physician in its entire history of nearly two centuries. Its nearest hospital is 2000 kilometres away in Papeete, Tahiti.)

Even more welcome than the arrival of the doctor on Pitcairn was that of an order placed months before – for a gallon of mayonnaise.

This was the first official personal contact between the two islands since 1864, and the visiting pilgrims and ship's crew almost doubled the population of Pitcairn. The pilgrims were able to spend six days on the island. But you may not be so lucky — permission must be obtained from Her Majesty's representative in New Zealand and he must first ascertain whether the Pitcairn Council agrees. Alternatively, you could try to get passage on one of the Scandinavian cargo ships which supply the island with essentials such as medical supplies two or three times a year.

To sail there alone, you would need to be a Chichester as you would be seeking a 1.75 square mile speck in the seventy million square miles that is the Pacific.

Pitcairn is more than 2000 kilometres from Tahiti, 3000 from Raratonga, 4000 from Panama, gateway to Europe, and 5000 from Auckland.

Visitors still find landing at the tiny cove, known as 'Bounty Bay', an adventure, even though the longboat that ferries them is now engine-powered. The boat pitches in the waves, rising to a crest, falling into a trough, until the right moment for entry through the surf is chosen when, at a centuries-old shout, the helmsman grasps the sweep and the boat plunges into the channel.

From the landing, one must still struggle up the Hill of Difficulty to reach Adamstown. The buildings around the square are maintained with pride but beyond it they are deserted and rotting. Of 70 house sites, only 20 are in use.

The *Bounty*'s Bible is still in the church and her anchor is in the town square, but few other relics remain. Some are believed to exist only six feet underwater but safe diving requires a perfect sea, and a perfect sea is something that comes along once in a century. Each January, a rough model of the historic ship is built and, on the 23rd, it is ritually torched in Bounty Bay.

The community is still loyal to Britain though her first official flag was a long time in coming; it was hoisted on 19th May, 1984, by

† *A few weeks after she safely returned the pilgrims to Mangareva, the 'Taporo II' ran aground on a reef on the island of Nukutarake in the Tuamotu group.*

Left: Over half the Pitcairn population

Governor Sir Richard Stratton, visiting from New Zealand. It flies bravely today over Adamstown square, close to the church bell, the true voice of Pitcairn. Upon this bell, various combinations of strokes signal a call to prayer or to work or, most exciting of all, to down tools and rush to the landing to greet an arriving ship.

In preparation for this rare event, an average Pitcairner will spend two days a week making souvenirs, hand-carved from wood which is collected on Henderson Island, 160 kilometres away. Each house has its lathe, chisels, axes, gouges, planes and sandpaper for the fashioning of objects such as flying fish, inlaid boxes and, of course, models of the *Bounty*. The women paint shells and turn pandanus leaf into hats and baskets.

For the rest of the week, one or two days will be spent cultivating vegetables, one fishing, one attending to the boats, half a day in public work, half a day at leisure and the Sabbath at rest.

Rates for the odd government job are one New Zealand dollar per hour, for skilled or unskilled work. The Island Magistrate earns a little over A$1,000 per year. Philately is the trade which saves the island from dying. Proceeds from stamp sales are managed by Britain and carefully doled out but this does not reduce the need for subsistence farming and trading.

Most islanders eat only two meals a day, a breakfast of soup and bread around 10 a.m., and a substantial 'tea' when work is done. They rarely drink and, with the exception of one brave person, never smoke. (In 1983, a law was finally passed enabling the importation of alcohol but was rescinded a month later.) They make occasional trips to neighbouring islands where they astonish onlookers by wading in water swarming with sharks, grabbing them by the tail and hurling them ashore. They retain their physical and mental capacities to an advanced age. People in their eighties toil in the fields and in 1983 one octogenarian, Edward Young, could still paddle his boat clear around the island in just over an hour.

The people are sustained in their precarious existence by a religious unity which is not quite so fervent as of yore. The entire island was converted to Seventh Day Adventism in 1887 by a United States missionary named John Tay.†

Mr. Tay made the islanders an offer too good to refuse: their grinding burden of guilt, made all the more difficult to bear as it was never discussed except in hymns that dwelt upon the fearful misdeeds of their forefathers, would be instantly lifted upon the Second Coming of Christ. The Church of England had never offered them a Christ they could feel and touch – Seventh Day Adventism promised this within their own lifetime.

A few sacrifices were entailed. Pork and crayfish had been the Pitcairners' two luxuries since 1789. As the swine 'cheweth not the cud', it was declared unclean. And as 'all that have not fins and scales shall be an abomination', it was goodbye to all shellfish – in particular, the mouth-watering spiny lobsters. In 1890, on the hundredth anniversary of their forefathers' landing, a mass ceremony was held in which the entire community was baptised. Every hog on the island, wild or domesticated, was rounded up and ritually slaughtered. The Adventism practised today is of a milder variety.

The place names of Pitcairn vividly recall

Above: Pitcairn wedding

its past. 'Matt's Rock' is remembered for the mutineer Matthew Quintal and 'McCoy's Valley' for his wild-eyed companion. 'Brown's Water', a sometimes dry spring which is one of only two sources of water but for rainfall, is named after William Brown, the *Bounty*'s assistant gardener.

'Down Under Johnnie Fall' is the place where the son of the mutineer John Mills fell fatally whilst gathering birds' eggs. 'Big Tree to Marae' goes back to the Polynesian temple site discovered by Christian on the day he landed. On that day Christian believed, as Captain Cook had believed of Norfolk, that here was 'a Paradise'. To today's Pitcairn children, it still is, although some of the adults are secretly close to despair. But help is at hand – or is it?

Arthur M. Ratliff, nicknamed 'Smiley' for unexplained reasons, claims he has the answer. Ratliff is a multimillionaire mine operator and real estate entrepreneur, who parlayed a $1500 loan into what is claimed to be a $100,000,000 fortune. Ratliff has made the Pitcairners an offer some find almost as difficult to refuse as that of John Tay. He will build them an $800,000 airstrip, he says, if the British Government will give him permission to live on nearby Henderson Island. But the Pitcairners are a mite cautious. Ratliff's religion is more fundamentalist than their own: it is Work. 'God didn't create us to play golf', he says, 'He created us to conquer the planet. He created us for victory!'

Though firmly informed by the British Government that its colony is not 'for sale', Mr. Ratliff continues to make overtures. Whether victory will eventually be his remains to be seen.

In the meantime, Pitcairn's survival may be only a little more likely than that of the sole Galapagos giant turtle who still suns himself on the Pitcairn rocks but has no mate with whom to breed.

† *Ironically, the Pitcairners had celebrated the Sabbath on a Saturday for their first 34 years due to Christian's failure to correct the calendar after crossing the dateline. This was the same error which caused his son to be christened 'Friday October'.*

Above left: Motorised tricycle – Pitcairn's most popular form of transport
Left: Looking down on the Landing Place from the Hill of Difficulty

APPENDIX 2

Pitcairn's Laws

No. 1 – Laws and Regulations of Pitcairn's Island

The Magistrate is to convene the public on occasions of complaints being made to him; and, on hearing both sides of the question, commit it to a jury.

He is to see all fines levied, and all public works executed; and every one must treat him with respect.

He is not to assume any power or authority on his own responsibility, or without the consent of the majority of the people.

A public journal shall be kept by the Magistrate, and shall from time to time be read; so that no one shall plead ignorance of the law for any crime he may commit. The journal shall be submitted to the inspection of those captains of British men-of-war, which occasionally touch at the island.

No. 2 – Laws for Dogs

If any one's dog is found chasing a goat, the owner of that dog shall pay a fine of one dollar and a half; one dollar to the owner of the goat or goats, and the other half to the informer.

If any dog kills or otherwise injures a goat, the owner of the dog so offending must pay the damages; but should suspicion rest on no particular dog, the owners of dogs generally must pay the damage. The foregoing law is of no effect when the goat or goats are upon cultivated land.

Persons who have fowls or hogs in the bush may take dogs to hunt them, but should the dogs commit damage during the hunt, the person taking the dogs to hunt must pay the damage.

No. 3 – Law for Cats

If any person under the age of ten years shall kill a cat, he or she shall receive corporal punishment. If any one, between the ages of ten and fifteen, kill a cat, he or she shall pay a fine of twenty-five dollars; half the fine to be given to the informer, the other half to the public. All masters of families convicted of killing a cat shall be fined fifty dollars; half of the fine to be given to the informer, the other half to the public.

N.B. Every person, from the age of fifteen upwards, shall pay a fine similar to masters of families.

No. 4 – Laws for Hogs

If a pig does any damage, the person who sustains the damage may take the pig so trespassing, no matter whether he sees the pig committing damage, or another person see the pig committing damage.

If any person or persons, see a pig, or pigs, committing damage, and neglect to inform the person sustaining the damage, the person guilty of such neglect must pay the damage.

No. 5 -- Law Regarding the School

There must be a school kept, to which all parents shall be obliged to send their children, who must previously be able to repeat the alphabet, and be of the age of from six to sixteen.

Mr. Nobbs shall be placed at the head of the school, assisted by such persons as shall be named by the Chief Magistrate.

The school hours shall be from seven o'clock in the morning until noon, on all days except Saturdays and Sundays, casualties and sickness excepted.

One shilling, or an equivalent as marked

Left: Root of a banyan, a tree Pitcairn and Norfolk share

below, shall be paid for each child per month, by the parents, whether the child attend School or not. In case Mr. Nobbs does not attend, the Assistant appointed by the Chief Magistrate shall receive the salary in proportion to the time Mr. Nobbs is away.

Equivalent for money:

One Barrel of Yams	8 shillings ($2)
One Barrel of Sweet Potatoes	8 shillings ($2)
One Barrel of Irish Potatoes	12 shillings ($3)
Three good Bunches of Plantains	4 shillings ($1)
One Day's Labour	2 shillings ($½)

The Chief Magistrate is to see the labour is well performed; and goods which may be given for money, shall be delivered, either at the market-place, or at the house of Mr. Nobbs, as he may direct.

No. 6 – Miscellaneous

If any person wants to cultivate any lands, he is to give notice of it to the public; and any person wanting any wood is to go on the aforesaid land and get it. If any person cuts more wood than is sufficient to build his house, the wood that remains after his house is finished is to be given to the next person who may want it to build a house. This extends only to the mero and borou timber.

Any person who may want any trees to break off the wind from his plantations or houses, is to make it known; and no one is allowed to cut them down, even if they be upon his own land.

At any meeting which may take place, there shall be no bringing up things that are past to criminate others, with a view to prevent justice with the case before the magistrate. Any one doing so will be punished by such a fine as a jury may think proper to award.

The Magistrate is to appoint church-wardens, four in number, beginning on the first of every month.

Any person detected in shooting or in any way killing white birds (unless it be sick) shall, for each bird that is killed, pay a dollar.

No. 7 – Laws for Wood

If any person goes to cut logs, to enclose a piece of ground, or any other purpose, he is not to cut any fit for building a dwelling house. The Magistrate is to appoint four men to inspect the logs after they are brought home; and should any be found serviceable for building dwelling-houses, they are to be taken from him and given to the next person who builds a house.

The third year from the time a person commences cutting wood he is to pick a share of thatch for covering dwelling-houses.

If the wood is left longer than the time specified, it is to be taken from him and given to the next person who builds a house.

Any person cutting logs, must not cut green ones until no more dry ones can be found. Any person without a pig-sty and wanting one, is allowed to cut green logs to make it with, if dry logs are not to be found.

No person is allowed to cut down any trees for logs and on which there are young ones growing, which may become serviceable for building in the future.

Any person having a large enclosure round his pig-sty, cutting down any tree on which there is any good logs, is not allowed to take the logs, but he is to leave it for the benefit of those who have no enclosure. He is also bound to inform those who have no enclosure where the logs are to be found; but if they do not cut them at the end of two weeks, any one may be allowed to cut them, and keep them for such service as they please. No one may cut green logs to repair his large enclosure, save what he may find on trees which have been cut and left above two weeks.

No. 8 – Laws respecting Landmarks

On the first day of January, after the Magistrate is elected, he shall assemble all those who should be deemed necessary; and with them he is to visit all landmarks that are upon the island, and replace those that are lost. Should anything occur to prevent its accomplishment in the time specified (the 1st of January), the Magistrate is bound to see it done the first opportunity.

No. 9 – Laws for Trading with Ships

No person or persons shall be allowed to get spirits of any sort from any vessel, or sell it to strangers or any person upon the island. Any one found guilty of so doing shall be punished by fine, or such other punishment as a jury shall determine on. No intoxicating liquor whatever shall be allowed to be taken on shore, unless it be for medical purposes. Any person found guilty of transgressing this law, shall be severely punished by a jury.

No females are allowed to go on board a foreign vessel, of any size or description, without the permission of the Magistrate; and in case the Magistrate does not go on board himself; he is to appoint four men to look after the females.

No. 10 – Law for the Public Anvil, &c.

Any person taking the public anvil and public sledge-hammer from the blacksmith's shop is to take it back after he has done with it; and in case the anvil and sledge-hammer should get lost by his neglecting to take it back, he is to get another anvil and sledge-hammer, and pay a fine of four shillings.

PLAN
OF
✳ NORFOLK ISLAND ✳
Shewing Grants and Subdivision
Scale 1 Inch   12 Chains

APPENDIX 3

Who Owns Norfolk Island?

The 'Paper of Cession' which the Pitcairners stoutly maintained had been handed to their forebears in 1856 finally turned up.

It was found in the Auckland Museum amongst the papers of Bishop Selwyn. It had apparently been in his possession in Norfolk, taken by him to the Solomons when the Mission migrated there, and subsequently to New Zealand.

Though it is not a document of total cession, it makes perfectly clear the intention of the Crown: it was to give all of the island bar about 900 acres, to the Pitcairners. There is absolutely no doubt that, at the time of their departure for Norfolk on the *Morayshire*, its Commander believed and told the Pitcairners that the entire island was to belong to them.

True, there had been a letter written to them by the British Consul, B.T. Nicholas, on 5th July, 1854, which denied this. Whilst assuring them that 'it is not at present intended to allow any other class of settlers to reside or occupy land on the island', it went on to say: 'I am at the same time to acquaint you that you will be pleased to understand that Norfolk Island *cannot be ceded*† to the Pitcairn islanders'.

This letter has been much quoted by people who believe the islanders were telling fibs. However, what they have overlooked is that the letter was written *almost two years before the exodus.*

A letter subsequently discovered throws new light on the subject. This was a despatch from Sir William Dennison to Sir George Grey, written *just two months before the departure of the 'Morayshire'*:

. . . the Islanders themselves have placed a magistrate in authority and are disposed to submit to his decisions. The effect, therefore, of placing any person on the Island vested with powers emanating either from Her Majesty or from the Governor of any of the adjacent colonies would be to generate parties, and lead to a disruption of ties which at present unite the community in one family. **I therefore wish to withdraw my former recommendation.**†
. . . You will see that I have directed him (Her Majesty's representative, Mr. Gregorie) to make but few reserves for public purposes, and with these exceptions, to **divide the whole Island between the newcomers.**†

He went on to recommend that the Governor General of the Australian colonies 'might have a *nominal jurisdiction*† in order that the people might have somebody to whom they might make their wants known'.

I believe this would have been the gist of what Acting Lieutenant Gregorie conveyed to the Pitcairners on the eve of their exodus. This is apparent in the conclusion of a Royal Commission into the matter which, whilst finding that the promises made were 'without the sanction of the Government and certainly not binding on the Crown', used these defensive words:

Whatever was conveyed to the original Islanders by the Officers who supervised their removal, and which might have given rise to the

† *My emphasis*

Far left: Plan of Norfolk Island showing grants and subdivision, 1887
Above: The Australian and Norfolk flags, symbolic of a once uneasy alliance, now perhaps mellowing

Top: *Sign on Quality Row*
Above: *Headstone of 'First Fleeter'*
convict in Norfolk Cemetery
Right: *'The Officers' Baths'*

belief that the Island was to be their exclusive property, etc.

Those words clearly suggest that the Crown knew what the Pitcairners had been promised.

I think it can reasonably be assumed that this despatch was received and approved of by the authorities because, on the 24th of June, 1856, an Order of Council, following an Act of Parliament, severed Norfolk from Van Diemen's Land and created it *a distinct and separate settlement.*

This was 16 days after the landing of the Pitcairners on Norfolk. On this day, Captain Fremantle, after consultation with Governor Dennison, read a proclamation 'To the Chief Magistrate of the Pitcairn Islanders':

All arrangements made by the community of Pitcairn Islanders as to the distribution of the land on Norfolk Island are to be subject to the approval of H.E. Sir W.T. Dennison, Governor Gen'l of N.S.W. The whole of the coastline including the jetties and the roads now made thro'out the Island are to be reserved as public property. The following buildings are also to be retained as belonging to H.M. Government. The gaol, The Government House, The Chaplain's House. Also 200 acres of cleared land at Longridge for a glebe and 500 acres elsewhere.

Previous writers have believed that this constituted a change of heart by Governor Dennison but I suggest that if the proclamation is read in conjunction with his letter to Sir George Grey, it would appear that his intent, at this stage, had not changed at all. The opening paragraph simply ensured that the land would be distributed under proper supervision and the rest of the text limits the claims of the Crown to

an area of about 900 acres.†

The balance of the island – almost 8000 acres – was to belong to the Pitcairners. This would have been sufficient reason for the Mission to confiscate the document (as seems likely) and thus not jeopardise the grant of land made to it. In the event, grants of 50 acres were made to each Pitcairn family and to several of their descendants.

It was on a subsequent visit that Governor Dennison changed his mind. He was highly displeased with the use to which the Pitcairners were putting the land and buildings he had risked his career to obtain for them. He apparently overlooked the fact that of the 194 who had arrived in 1856 there were only about 50 able-bodied men. It could hardly be expected that these people, especially with their Polynesian work ethic, could maintain an island which had required the forced labour of over 1000 convicts.

The Governor had found it easy to be beneficient in absentia, but on meeting the Pitcairners he found they did not fit his mental picture. He was distressed to note 'an undue

development of Tahitian blood'. 'I wished', he said, 'to bring out more of the Englishman'.

From this time on, further grants were rare and in the end *less than half* of the island was passed on to the Pitcairners. However, the right to self-government was honoured for forty years, albeit subject to much harassment from the mainland Governors. This right was withdrawn in 1896 when the Governor of the day, Viscount Hampden, from his ivory tower in New South Wales, decided that the islanders were incapable of governing themselves. I believe he set forth for Norfolk with his mind made up and, in what now reads as a pompous and ill-informed speech, abolished all Norfolk Island Laws (illegally, according to many) and proclaimed new ones allocating total authority to New South Wales. And the traditional granting of free land to islanders on marriage was wiped out at a stroke.

Particularly resented and still remembered is the fact that the post of Chief Magistrate became an Australian appointment and was never again held by an islander.

The bitterest humiliation of all came in 1908 when Governor Sir Harry Rawson demanded that islanders resident in Kingston buildings – to which their parents had been handed the keys – should abnegate all ownership rights or be evicted. Most were. A number of the evicted people set fire to their homes that night and the evidence is to be seen to this day in Quality Row.

In 1914, Britain relinquished her authority over the island and handed over control to Australia. Simultaneously, a large number of Norfolk Islanders enlisted to fight and die for the Empire. Many of them did. It is important to note that Norfolk was not *annexed* to Australia

then or since, despite very considerable pressures from that country that this should be done.

In 1965, Australia's power to make laws for Norfolk was challenged by a resident of thirty years, Mr. H.S. Newbury. He conducted his own case, lost, and was refused the right to appeal.

In 1976, a Royal Commission was set up to determine whether Australia should abandon Norfolk and, if not, what would be the islanders'

† *500 acres plus 200 acres at Longridge and a further area of approximately 200 acres occupied by the gaol and other buildings.*

Below left: The Salt Mill, overlooking Emily Bay
Bottom left: The original Norfolk Cemetery
Above: The Commissariat Store, now used as a church

constitutional rights. Its conclusions were contained in a famous, or infamous, document known as the 'Nimmo Report'. It recommended that the island should be integrated into Australia, be given a token vote (as a sub-division of the A.C.T.) and be forced to accept two things which the vast majority of its inhabitants believed they needed like a hole in the head — Australian welfare and Australian taxes.

Had Sir John Nimmo's recommendations been accepted, a calamitous loss of the islanders' sense of identity would inevitably have followed. Some insight into Sir John's attitude may be gained from his remark at the time: 'The island offers a pleasant holiday venue for Australians and New Zealanders, but if it sank into the Pacific following an earthquake, intending holiday-makers would soon find an alternative'.

A request from the Norfolk Island Council for a referendum was rejected by the Minister (Senator Withers) on the grounds that it would be 'time-consuming and costly'. (It could have been carried out in six weeks at a cost of $300.)

In 1977, the Norfolk Island Council presented a well-documented appeal to the United Nations that the island should not be absorbed against the wishes of its people. The United Nations Association of Australia, following a thorough analysis of the situation, described Canberra's stance as 'patently ludicrous'.

On a matter of protocol, the appeal was unable to be processed but it apparently had an effect on Australia's conscience as, somewhat to the astonishment of the locals, Parliament passed the Norfolk Island Act under which its people regained some measure of self-

Below: Gallows Gate
Bottom: 1833 headstone bearing initials only

government with a promise of more to come should they demonstrate some measure of 'responsibility'.

Since then, the Australian Government has overridden three important Acts passed by the Norfolk Island Assembly. Australia has installed its own system of voting, denied intending residents living on the island a vote (since rescinded) and refused to allow automatic residency rights to people of Pitcairn descent.

There are other anomalies arising from the confusion as to whether the island belongs to itself or to Australia. An Australian school-teacher, David Lewis, whose term of appointment on the island (with which he had fallen in love) had expired, unsuccessfully challenged Australia's constitutional right to deport him. The enormous stress he suffered in his lone endeavour to establish a legal basis for his defence finally resulted in some bizarre actions.

The David Lewis story is a fascinating one which I hope to tell in detail, with his co-operation, one day. Threats to blow up the Administration buildings and to take over the island cannot be condoned but must not be allowed to obscure the strong logical points Lewis made. One of the anomalies he pointed out to me, which Australia consistently refuses to address, will continue to rankle until it does.

It concerns 933 acres — one-ninth of the island — which should have been returned to the people of Norfolk Island when the Melanesian Mission pulled out. The Mission was paid for the land with money lying in a trust fund established in 1852 by a group of well-to-do British-based members of the Church of England 'for the benefit of the Pitcairn Islanders'. The Fund was subsequently added to from local sources. The title to this land somehow went to, and is still held by, Australia.

I have unearthed a mass of documents in the Canberra archives (bearing, amongst other signatures, those of John Curtin and J.B. Chifley, the then Prime Minister and his successor) which make it clear that the Mission did not transfer the land to the Commonwealth of Australia and special legislation was introduced to effect this. From counsel's opinion it appears that the Pitcairners were pressuring Australia to acquire the land and then make it available to their young people; hence, perhaps, the application of Norfolk monies. I believe the young people are still waiting.

But what about the rest of Norfolk Island?

The United Nations Association of Australia believes that Norfolk is officially a territory *under the authority* of Australia, but certainly not a *Territory of Australia*. The nearest one can get to an official 'owner' is a mythical body called The Crown, although the British monarchy lays no claims to it whatsoever. So it appears that Norfolk cannot legally be absorbed into Australia against the wishes of a majority of its people.

A fairly vocal minority would like to see Norfolk totally integrated into Australia, mainly for imagined welfare benefits. Another, principally composed of Pitcairn descendants, stands for total independence, claiming that it is entirely due to their Polynesian-imbued tolerance that the removal of their bounty has not led to another mutiny. I think history is on their side. And what all Norfolk residents can learn from it is that we should be ever vigilant lest we be swallowed up by Australia and reduced to a suburb of Canberra.

Given that, I believe that the cynicism of many is gradually mellowing as a realisation grows that such things as the Australian-maintained airport, which allows a two-and-a-half hour flight to the mainland instead of a five-day boat journey, are not all that hard to take. Australia is financing the restoration of many of the buildings which are part of its and Norfolk's heritage and is also offering much valuable help in turning the Mount Pitt area into a properly managed National Park. It has recently offered, on a quid pro quo basis, $2,000,000 for a sewage scheme. In mid-1985, it handed over more rights to the local Assembly.

Beyond all these material things, some Pitcairners are reminding themselves that the granting of 50 acres of land to every original Pitcairn family (an area much bigger than Pitcairn), plus the use of very substantial buildings, and the provision of quite massive stores and utensils, constituted perhaps the most generous gesture in the history of the British Empire.

If Britain can turn the other cheek, maybe Norfolk can do the same to Australia. Everybody needs a friend. Certainly, Norfolk residents must continue to make it clear to Australia that they will not be treated as pawns. But, simultaneously, I believe they will try harder to communicate the idea that they genuinely appreciate her help.

Provided Australia allows Norfolk a decent level of self-government, I think the community will be happy to live by George Hunn Nobbs's words of a hundred years ago:

The land is a goodly land, and needs nothing but a contented mind, a persevering spirit and a grateful heart to render it productive and pleasant.

Top: Crudely chiselled headstone, probably from the First Settlement
Above: Steps to the old Civil Hospital

Next spread: Emily Bay, serene amongst the whitecaps

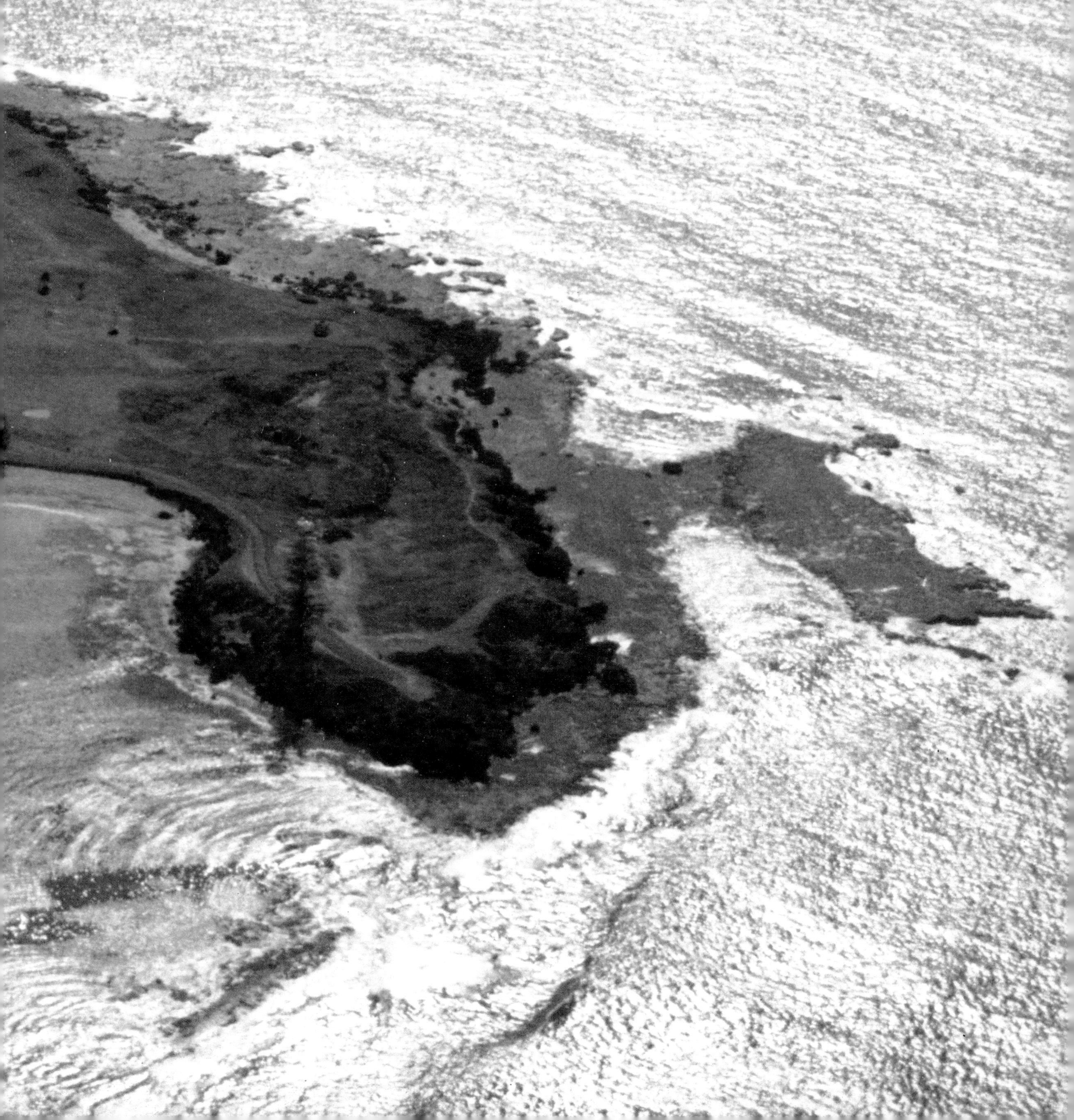

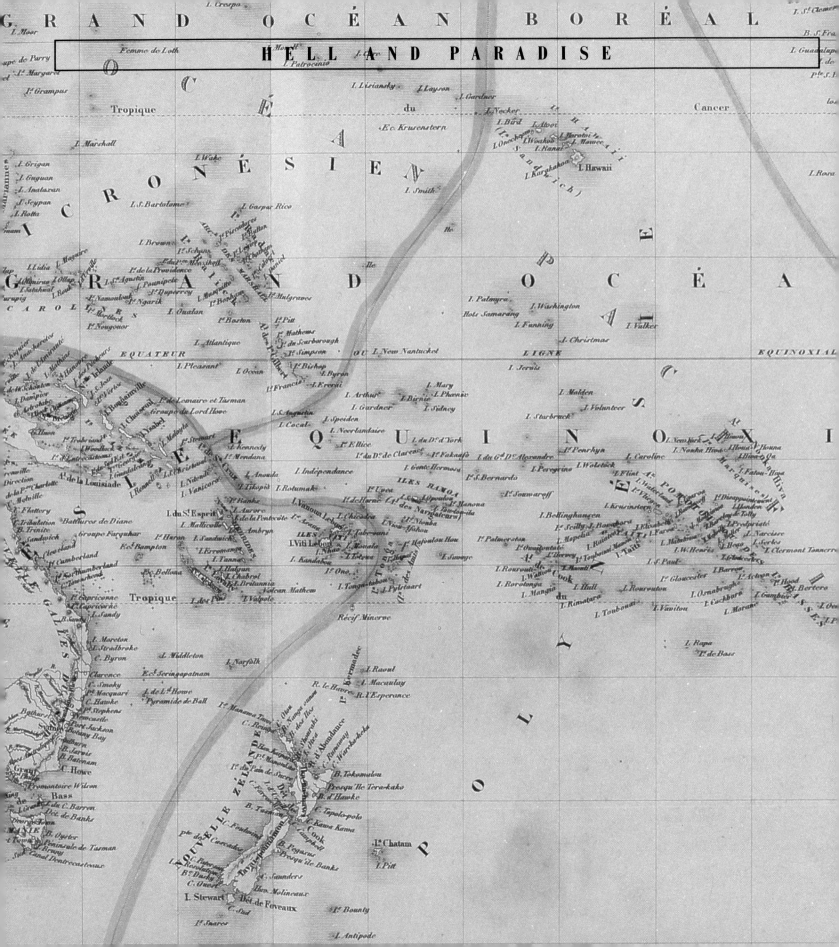

Books and Manuscripts Consulted

Adams, John: Autographed narrative given to Captain Beechey in 1825 (Mitchell Library)

Ball, Ian M.: *Pitcairn: Children of the Bounty* 1974

Barrow, Sir John: *Eventful History of the Mutiny and Piratical Seizure of H.M.S. Bounty* 1831

Barry, J.V.: *Alexander Maconochie of Norfolk Island* 1958

Barry, J.V.: *The Life and Death of John Price* 1964

Becke, Louis, and Jeffery, Walter: *The Mutineer: A Romance of Pitcairn Island* 1898

Beechey, F.W.: *Narrative of a Voyage to the Pacific and Beering's Strait* 1831

Best, Ensign: Journal 1837-43

Bligh, William: *A Narrative of the Mutiny on Board His Majesty's Ship Bounty* 1790

Britts, M.G.: *The Commandants* 1980

Carteret, Philip: *A Voyage Round the Globe 1766-9* 1823

Cash, Martin: *A Personal Narrative* ... 1911 reprint

Chauvel, Charles: *In the Wake of the Bounty* Filmscript, 1933

Chichester, Francis: *The Lonely Sea and the Sky* 1964

Christian, Edward: *A Short Reply to Captain William Bligh's Answer* 1795

Christian, Glynn: *A Fragile Paradise* 1984

Clarke, Marcus: *For the Term of His Natural Life* 1874

Clarke, Marcus: *Memorial Volume* 1884

Clune, Frank: *The Norfolk Island Story* 1967

Colonial Office: Various correspondence

Cook, Captain James: *Journals* Various

Cook, Thomas: *The Exile's Lamentations* 1841-4, published 1978

Dalkin, R. Nixon: *Colonial Era Cemetery of Norfolk Island* 1981

Danielsson, Bengt: *What Happened on the Bounty* 1962

Eldershaw, M.B.: *The Life and Times of Captain John Piper* 1973

Folger, Mayhew: Log of the *Topaz* 1807-9 Quoted in R.B. Nicolson's *The Pitcairners*

Gazzard, Albert: *The Bounty and After* 1943

Hawkesworth, John: *An Account of the Voyages ... for making Discoveries in the Southern Hemisphere* 1773

Hazzard, Margaret: *Commandants and Convicts of Norfolk Island 1788-1855* 1978

Hill, Joshua: *Memorandum* 1841 (Dixson Library)

Historical Records of Australia: Various

Historical Records of New South Wales: Various

Hoare, Merval: *Norfolk Island. An Outline of Its History 1774-1981* 1982

Hough, Richard: *Captain Bligh and Mr. Christian* 1979 (published as *The Bounty* 1984)

Humble, Richard: *Captain Bligh* 1976

Marrington, Pauline: *In the Sweet Bye and Bye* 1981

Maude, H.E.: 'In Search of a Home', *Journal of the Polynesian Society* 1958

Left: Map of the Pacific taken from A. R. Fremlin's 'Océanie', circa 1820

Minutes of the Proceedings of the Court-martial . . . on ten persons charged with mutiny. . . 1794

Moerenhout, J.A.: *Voyages aux Iles du Grand Ocean* 1837

Nicolson, R.B.: *The Pitcairners* 1965

Nobbs, Christopher: *Which Future for Norfolk Island?* 1983

Nobbs, George Hunn: Papers (Mitchell Library)

Nimmo, Sir John: *Report of Royal Commission on Norfolk Island* 1976

Nordhoff, Charles, and Hall, James Norman: *The Bounty Trilogy* 1933-5

Park, Ruth, and Emmanuel, Cedric: *Norfolk Island and Lord Howe Island* 1982

Ramsay, Doctor: Scrap book of the log of the ship *Surry* Quoted in R.B. Nicolson's *The Pitcairners*

Selwyn, Bishop: Papers (Auckland Museum)

Ross, A.S.C.:*The Pitcairnese Language* 1964

Shapiro, Harry L.: *Heritage of the Bounty* 1936

Shillibeer, J.: *Narrative of the Briton's Voyage to Pitcairn's Island* 1817

Staines, Sir T., and Pipon, P.: *Interesting Report on the Only Remaining Mutineers of His Majesty's Ship Bounty, Resident on Pitcairn's Island in the Pacific Ocean* Undated

Stuart, R.P., and Naylor, T.B.: *The Botany Bay of Botany Bay* 1846, published 1979

Warren, Samuel: *The Paradise in the Pacific* 1855

Wilkinson, C.S.: *Wake of the Bounty* 1953

Wilson, Erle: *Adams of the Bounty* 1958

Wiseman, Bill, and Treloar, Bruce: *Living on Norfolk Island* 1975

Young, Rosalind: *Mutineers of the Bounty and Story of Pitcairn Island, 1790-1894* 1924

Index

Actaeon 127
Adams, John (alias Alexander Smith) 37, 43,
    45, 58, 59, 85, 89, 91-5, 99, 111-4, 119, 121,
    126
Adams, Rachel 111
Adamstown 93, 94, 95, 169, 170
Adventure Bay 41
Albion (later Sydney) see Sydney (New South
    Wales)
Anderson, Major Joseph 105, 108
Anson Bay 17, 104, 161
Auckland 168
Austral Islands 59

Ball's Pyramid 162
Banks, Sir Joseph 14, 19, 20, 35, 36, 77, 79, 94,
    131
Barney Duffy's Gulley 108
Barrow, stipendiary magistrate 136
Barrow, Sir John 21, 53, 119
Barry, J.V. 139
Bass, George 71
Batchelor, John 16, 17
Becke, Louis 85
Beechey, Captain F.W. 85, 111-3, 121
Betham, Richard 21
Big Tree to Marae 170
Bligh, Betsy (née Betham) 21, 24, 80
Bligh, Lieutenant (later Captain) William 17,
    19-26, 29, 34-6, 41-53, 55, 58-61, 64, 65,
    75, 77-81, 92, 93, 98-9, 112
Bligh's Cap 24
Blossom 111, 112
Bond, First Lieutenant Francis 25
Bond, Tom 25
Boswell, James 19
Botany Bay 9, 19, 74, 137
Bouganville, Louis Antoine de 34, 35
Bounty 5, 17, 19, 20, 24, 25, 29, 31, 34, 35, 37,
    41-6, 55, 58, 59, 60-1, 63, 65, 74, 83, 85,
    89, 94, 95, 122, 145, 170
Bounty Bay 113, 169
Bounty Bible 91, 169
Branka House 147
Brisbane, Sir Thomas 103
Britannia 28
Briton 43, 94, 98

Brown William ('Illiam Dhone') 27
Brown, William 59, 83, 85, 89, 171
Brown's Water 171
Buffett, John 111, 113-5, 119, 122; 123, 126
Bunker, Noah 114-5, 118
Burne-Jones, Sir Edward Coley 152
Burkett, Thomas 43, 45, 46, 64, 65
Burton, Judge 106
Byrne, Michael 64
Byron Bay 16
Byron, John 28

Campbell, Dr. Neil 21
Campbell, Duncan 24
Camperdown, battle of 78
Cape Horn 31, 36, 37
Cape of Good Hope 31
Cape Town 41
Cape York 65
Carteret, Philip 28, 59
Cascade Bay 67, 74, 157, 162
Cash, Martin 133, 136
Castlereagh, Viscount 81
Cemetery Bay 167
Cerini, Dr. James 85
Chichester, Sir Francis 162-3, 168
Chifley, J.B. 181
Childs, Major 133, 137
Chimney Hill 167
Christian, Charles 29
Christian, Edward 27, 77, 78, 94
Christian, Fletcher 19, 25-9, 36-7, 41-7, 55-61,
    64, 83-9, 94, 95, 171
Christian, Glynn 29, 91
Christian, Mary 113
Christian, Thursday (previously Friday)
    October I 43, 92-5, 113, 122, 171
Christian, Thursday October II 147
Christian's Cave 84, 89
Churchill, Charles 43, 45, 64, 79, 119
Clarke, Marcus 139-43
Cockatoo Island 139
Cockermouth 26
Coleman, Joseph 45, 64
Coleridge, S.T. 27, 84, 85
Comet 122
Commerson, Philibert 34
Cook, Captain James 9, 10, 14, 21, 24, 28, 34,
    35, 36, 55, 67, 71, 91, 171
Cook Islands 59
Copenhagen, battle of 79
Coupang 52-3, 65

Crescent 21
Crook, Rev. William Pascoe 121
Curtin, John 181
Cyrus 111

Daedalus 71
Dampier, William 19
Dannebroge 79
Darling, General Sir Ralph 103
Davey, Dr. John 168
Dawes, Rufus (hero of Marcus Clarke's *For the
    Term of His Natural Life)* 109, 142-3
Denham, Captain 146
Dennison, Sir William 127, 147, 177, 178
Difficulty, Hill of 60, 95, 145, 169
Director 78
Doherty, Dennis 137
Donaldson, Captain Vance 103-4
Down Under Johnnie Fall 171
Duffy, Barney 107-8
Dulcie Island 65
Duncan, Admiral 78

Edge, The 60
Edwards, Captain Edward 64-5
Elcum, Rev. 160
Elephant 79
Ellison, Thomas 43, 64, 65
Emily Bay 17, 104, 157, 161, 162, 167
Endeavour Straits 42
Eurydice 28
Evans, John 111, 123, 126, 127
Ewanrigg (Cumberland) 26

ffrench, Jemima 115
Fiji Islands 59
Flinders, Matthew 71
Folger, Captain Mayhew 43, 92-3, 94, 98
Forster, George 14
Foveaux, Major 72-3, 74, 81
Frazier, John 79
Fremantle, Captain 178
Friendly Islands 41
Fryer, John 52
Fyans, Captain 'Flogger' 105

Gambier Islands 126, 168
Garth, Edward 16
Gasgoin, Olivia 16
Gauguin, Paul 36, 42, 152
Gazzard, Albert 147
Gilbert, George 35

Gillocrist, the Norse 26
Gipps, Governor of New South Wales 133
Goff, Black John 104
Gough, Susannah 16
Graham, surgeon 143
Great Barrier Reef 51, 65
Gregorie, Lieutenant 177
Grey, Sir George 177, 178
Grimshaw, Beatrice 153-6

Hall, Captain John 111
Hampden, Viscount 179
Hango Hill 27
Hawkesbury (river) 71
Hayes, Sir Henry Brown 74
Headstone 108
Heffernan, trooper 107-8
Henderson Island 170-1
Hermes, Neil 69
Heywood, Midshipman (later Admiral) Peter
    63-5, 77-8, 85, 119
Hill, Joshua 122-7, 145
Hillibrant, Henry 64
Hobart Town 92, 131, 137
Hood, Admiral 28
Howe, Admiral 28
Hume, David 21
Hunter 21
Hunter, Captain John 67, 71

Indefatigable 115
Inett, Ann 16
Isle of Man 21, 26, 27, 55
Isobella see Mauatua

Jacky-Jacky see Westwood
Jacky-Jacky (peak) 104
Jamison, surgeon 16
Johnson, Dr. Samuel 19

Kavenagh (a member of Martin Cash's
    gang) 136
Kealakekua Bay 24
Kimberley, Edward 73
King, Lieutenant Philip Gidley 10, 14, 16, 17,
    59, 67, 71, 80
King, Second Lieutenant C. 24
Kingston (Norfolk) 14, 17, 74, 167, 168

La Perouse 11, 59
Lady Nelson 75, 77, 80
Lady Sinclair 80

Landing Place 60, 95
Laws, Commander 121
Lewis, David 180
London Missionary Society 121
Lord Howe Island 68, 162
Lucas, Nathaniel 16
Lucy Ann 122

McArthur, John 80
McCoy, William 43, 59, 83, 89, 171
McCoy's Valley 171
McCrystyn, Deemster John 26
McLennan, Charles 11, 16, 143
M'Intosh, Thomas 64
Maconochie, Alexander 131-3
Malmsbury, Joseph 73
Mangareva 168
Mareva 83
Martin, Isaac 43, 58, 83, 85, 89
Martin, Jenny 58
Matavai Bay 31
Matt's Rock 171
Mauatua 37, 43, 55
Maude, Professor H.E. 37
Maude, Mrs. H.E. 93
Melanesian Mission 151-2, 177, 178, 180
Melville, Herman 36, 42, 152
Menallee 83, 89
Mercury 59
Michener, James 163
Mills, John 43, 45, 83, 85, 89, 170
Millward, John 64, 65
Mi'Mitti see Mauatua
Moerenhout, Captain Antoine 114, 118-9,
    122, 123
'Moira' 115
Moorea 58
Moorland Close (Cumbria) 25
Morayshire 146, 177
Morisset, Commandant J.T. 81, 104-5
Morrison, James 64
Mount Pitt 10, 17, 68, 139, 181
Muspratt, William 43, 64

Napoleon 93, 94, 104, 126
Nelson, Admiral Horatio 79, 94
Nepean Island 14
New Caledonia 9, 10, 16
New South Wales 14, 16, 103, 113, 115, 131, 151,
    178, 179
New Zealand 9, 10, 14, 16, 161, 169, 170, 177
Newbury, H.S. 179

Nicholas, B.T. 177
Nimmo Report 180
Nimmo, Sir John 180
Nobbs, Fletcher Christian 147
Nobbs, George Hunn 114-8, 119, 123, 126, 127,
    145-7, 151, 161, 168, 173-4, 181
Nobbs, Isaac 118
Nomuka see Friendly Islands
Norfolk, Duchess of 9
Norfolk (first child born on the island) 16
Norfolk Island 5, 9-17, 24, 46, 59, 61, 67-75, 80,
    81, 93, 99, 103-9, 127, 130-7, 139-43, 146-7,
    151-68, 177-81
Norfolk Island Laws 179
Norfolk Ridge 10
Norfolk (sloop) 71
Norman, Charles 64
Nott, Rev. Henry 121
Nukuturake 169

Otaheite/Otaheyte see Tahiti

Pandora (1790) 64, 65
Pandora (1849) 145
Pandora's Box 64-5
Papeete 122, 168
Parker, Commander-in-Chief 79
Patteson, John Coleridge 152
Pease, Mrs. Parnell 157
Phillip, Captain Arthur 9, 10, 14, 16
Phillip (later Philip) Island 14, 69, 71, 104
Phillips, Lieutenant Molesworth 24
Piper, Captain John 73-5, 81
Pipon, Captain 94-5, 98
Pitcairn Island 5, 43, 59-61, 83-4, 85, 89, 91-9,
    111-9, 121-7, 145-7, 168-71
Pitcairn Laws 127, 173-5
Point Piper 74
Point Ross 67
Pomare 122, 127
Pomare Waheine 121
Porpoise 81
Port Arthur 131, 139, 143
Port Jackson 17, 80
Port Vila 162
'Potato Joe' see Anderson, Major Joseph
Price, John 104, 139, 142-3
Price, Sir Rose 139
Purcell, William 42, 43, 52

Quality Row 147, 167, 179
Queen Elizabeth's Lookout 167

Quintal, Charlotte 127
Quintal, Magistrate Edward 127
Quintal, Kitty 119
Quintal, Lucy Ann 122
Quintal, Matthew 37, 43, 45, 58, 59, 61, 83, 89, 119, 171

Raine, Captain Thomas 22
Ramsey, Dr. David 99
Ramsey, John 78
Ranger 21
Raratonga 168
Ratliff, Arthur M. ('Smiley') 171
Rawdon-Hastings, Francis, Marquis of Hastings, Earl of Moira 115
Rawson Hall 109
Rawson, Sir Harry 179
Resolution (Captain Cook's ship) 9, 24, 34
Resolution (intended escape-boat) 64
Resolution (Norfolk's trading schooner) 161
Rodney, Admiral 28
Rogers, Captain 29
Ross, Major Robert 67
Ross-haven 67
Rousseau, Jean-Jacques 94
Russell, Lord Edward 127

St. Barnabas Chapel 152
St. Kilda 147
Selwyn, Bishop 147, 152, 177
Shapiro, Harry L. 147
Shears, Mary Ann 74
Short, Captain Joseph 80
Sirius 5, 19, 61, 67
Skinner, Richard 64
Slaughter Bay 17, 168
Smith, Adam 21
Smith, Alexander see Adams, John
Society for the Propagation of the Gospel 145
Society Islands 59
Solomon Islands 177
South Australia 127
Spithead 29
Staines, Sir Thomas 98
Stevenson, Robert Louis 36, 42, 152
Stewart, George 64
Stratton, Sir Richard 170
Sully 58, 60, 83
Sumner, John 45, 64
Supply 11, 67
Surry 99
Sydney Bay 14

Sydney Cove 9, 80
Sydney (later Kingston) see Kingston (Norfolk)
Sydney, Lord 9
Sydney (New South Wales) 9, 74-5, 80, 105, 163
Sylph's Hole 162

Tahiti 17, 19, 31-9, 41, 43, 46, 55, 58, 64, 74, 91, 112, 121-2, 126, 127, 168
Taparo II 168, 169
Tararo 82
Targus 43, 94, 95
Tay, John 170, 171
Teimua 89
Teio, wife of John Adams 111, 113, 119
Tetaheite 89, 92
Therry, Sir Roger 105
Thompson, Matthew 64, 119
Timor 47, 52
Tinafanaea 83
Tofua 43, 46
Tonga Islands 59
Toobouai 55, 58
Toofaiti 83
Tookee 71
Topaz 81, 92
Townsend, Lord James 126
Townson, Captain 71
Trafalgar, battle of 79, 94
Trollope, Anthony 137
Tu, king 64
Tuamotu Islands 169
Turner, Charles 107-8
Turtle Bay see Emily Bay
Turton, Captain 103
Tynwald 26
Tynwald Hill 26

Ullathorne, Bishop 106-7, 132, 143

Van Diemen's Land 31, 41, 71, 74, 75, 81, 103, 113, 131, 143, 178
Vaucluse 74
Victoria 127, 143
Volador 114

Waldegrave, Captain William 119
Wallis, Samuel 28, 35
Warnham, trooper 107-8
Warrior 79
Wentworth, D'Arcy 74
Wentworth, William Charles 74
West Indies 19, 28, 37

Westwood, 'Jacky-Jacky' 104, 133, 136-7
Whitsunday Islands 52
Widdicombe, Richard 11
Wilkinson, Isaac 27
Williams, John (missionary) 59, 151
Williams, John (seaman) 43, 59, 83, 85, 88
Willson, Bishop 137
Wood, Captain 145
Woodoo 71
Wordsworth, William 27, 84
Wright, Thomas Saulsbury ('Tommy the Banker') 132

Young, Dolly 111
Young, Edward 43, 45, 83, 89, 91, 92, 122
Young, Edward (present-day descendant of the mutineer) 170
Young, Frederick 152
Young, Jemima 145
Young, Mary 147
Young, Simon 147
Young, Sir John 152
Young, Susannah 89, 92

Zebra 122

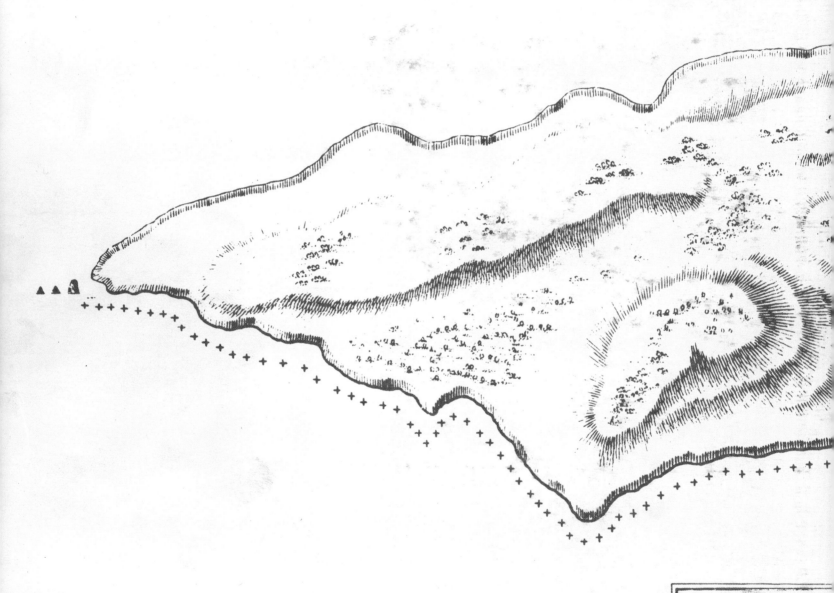

Coral Rock

20

24

24   24

25

25

A CHAR
OF PITCA
Latitude 25°